Wild Tales
Student Workbook | Part 2

A Demme Learning Publication

Wild Tales Student Workbook, Parts 1 and 2
©2019 Spelling You See
©2013 Karen J. Holinga, PhD
Published and distributed by Demme Learning

All rights reserved. No part of this book may be reproduced, stored in a retrieval system, or transmitted in any form by any means—electronic, mechanical, photocopying, recording, or otherwise—without prior written permission from Demme Learning.

spellingyousee.com

1-888-854-6284 or +1 717-283-1448 | demmelearning.com
Lancaster, Pennsylvania USA

ISBN 978-1-60826-607-4 (Wild Tales Student Workbook)
ISBN 978-1-60826-609-8 (Part 2)
Revision Code 0321

Printed in the United States of America by Innovative Technologies in Print.
 2 3 4 5 6 7 8 9 10

For information regarding CPSIA on this printed material call: 1-888-854-6284 and provide reference #0321-03042021

To the Instructor

This is the second half of the *Wild Tales* spelling program, designed to help your student become a confident and successful speller while spending only a few minutes each day on spelling practice. The program is not difficult, but it is different.

Even if you have successfully completed the first half of *Wild Tales* with your student, now is a good time to review your Instructor's Handbook, particularly the sections titled **Getting Started: A *Wild Tales* Week** and **About the Activities.** These sections include practical information about how to complete daily and weekly activites to provide the best opportunity for your student's success.

Be sure to check the lesson-by-lesson instructions in the Instructor's Handbook at the beginning of each lesson and discuss any new or unusual patterns that are introduced there. You will find specific tips about what to look for in each passage, complete chunking solutions, and the week's passage for dictation.

If you would like to have a more in-depth understanding of the philosophy of Spelling You See or the developmental stages of spelling, this information can be found at spellingyousee.com.

19A Vowel Chunks

See Lesson 19 in the Instructor's Handbook for instructions and tips.

Today's Activities:

☐ Shared reading   ☐ Chunking (<u>**vowel chunks**</u>)   ☐ Copywork

Some people use sponges to clean. Did you know that sponges are animals? They live in the ocean. They are attached to rocks or the sea floor. The sponge has holes that let in water. As the water flows through the holes, the sponge gets the food it needs to eat.

Vowel Chunks

aa	ae	ai	ao	au	aw	ay
ea	ee	ei	eo	ew	ey	eau
ia	ie	ii	io	iu		
oa	oe	oi	oo	ou	ow	oy
ua	ue	ui	uo	uy		

Wild Tales

Copywork

Copy the story on the lines below. Then mark the same letter patterns that you marked on the printed passage. Look at the previous page if you need help finding the chunks.

Some people use sponges

S

to clean. Did you know

t

that sponges are animals?

t

They live in the ocean.

T

Wild Tales **19A**

19B
Vowel Chunks

Today's Activities:

☐ Shared reading ☐ Chunking (**vowel chunks**) ☐ Copywork

Some people use sponges to clean. Did you know that sponges are animals? They live in the ocean. They are attached to rocks or the sea floor. The sponge has holes that let in water. As the water flows through the holes, the sponge gets the food it needs to eat.

Vowel Chunks

aa ae ai ao au aw ay

ea ee ei eo ew ey eau

ia ie ii io iu

oa oe oi oo ou ow oy

ua ue ui uo uy

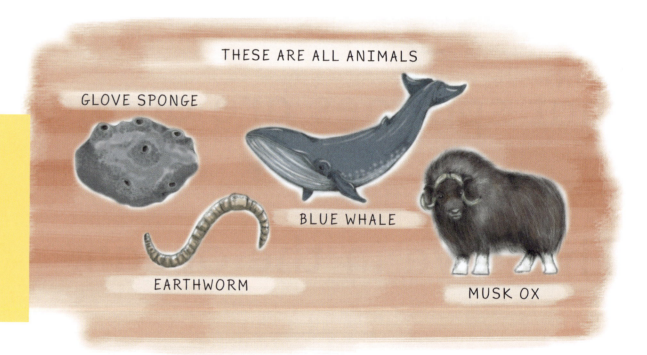

THESE ARE ALL ANIMALS

GLOVE SPONGE

BLUE WHALE

EARTHWORM

MUSK OX

Wild Tales

Copywork

Copy the story on the lines below. Then mark the same letter patterns that you marked on the printed passage. Look at the previous page if you need help finding the chunks.

They are attached to

T

rocks or the sea floor.

r

The sponge has holes

T

that let in water.

t

19C Vowel Chunks

Today's Activities:

☐ Shared reading   ☐ Chunking (<u>vowel chunks</u>)   ☐ Copywork

Some people use sponges to clean. Did you know that sponges are animals? They live in the ocean. They are attached to rocks or the sea floor. The sponge has holes that let in water. As the water flows through the holes, the sponge gets the food it needs to eat.

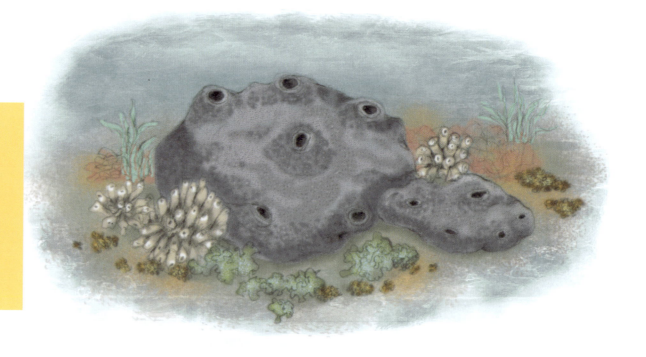

Vowel Chunks

aa	ae	ai	ao	au	aw	ay
ea	ee	ei	eo	ew	ey	eau
ia	ie	ii	io	iu		
oa	oe	oi	oo	ou	ow	oy
ua	ue	ui	uo	uy		

Wild Tales

Copywork

Copy the story on the lines below. Then mark the same letter patterns that you marked on the printed passage. Look at the previous page if you need help finding the chunks.

As the water flows

A

through the holes, the

t

sponge gets the food

s

it needs to eat.

i

19D Vowel Chunks

Today's Activities:

☐ Shared reading ☐ Chunking (**vowel chunks**) ☐ No Rule Day

Some people use sponges to clean. Did you know that sponges are animals? They live in the ocean. They are attached to rocks or the sea floor. The sponge has holes that let in water. As the water flows through the holes, the sponge gets the food it needs to eat.

Vowel Chunks

aa	ae	ai	ao	au	aw	ay
ea	ee	ei	eo	ew	ey	eau
ia	ie	ii	io	iu		
oa	oe	oi	oo	ou	ow	oy
ua	ue	ui	uo	uy		

Wild Tales

No Rule Day

Draw a picture of the story or write your own story. Be creative and have fun.

19E
Vowel Chunks

📖 See Lesson 19 in the Instructor's Handbook for instructions and tips.

Today's Activities:

☐ Shared reading   ☐ Chunking (<u>vowel chunks</u>)   ☐ Dictation

Some people use sponges to clean. Did you know that sponges are animals? They live in the ocean. They are attached to rocks or the sea floor. The sponge has holes that let in water. As the water flows through the holes, the sponge gets the food it needs to eat.

Vowel Chunks

aa	ae	ai	ao	au	aw	ay
ea	ee	ei	eo	ew	ey	eau
ia	ie	ii	io	iu		
oa	oe	oi	oo	ou	ow	oy
ua	ue	ui	uo	uy		

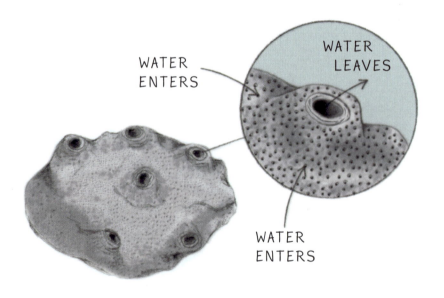

WATER FLOW THROUGH COMMON BATH SPONGE

Dictation

Turn the page to write this week's story from dictation.

Write this week's story from dictation. Take your time and ask for help if you need it.

Some

I spelled _____ words correctly.

20A Consonant Chunks

> See Lesson 20 in the Instructor's Handbook for instructions and tips.

Today's Activities:

☐ Shared reading   ☐ Chunking (**consonant chunks**)   ☐ Copywork

A sloth spends most of its life upside down. It hangs from a tree branch. The sloth digs its sharp claws into the branch and holds on tightly. The sloth eats leaves from the tree. Then it falls asleep upside down. It is hard to get a sloth to move from its tree!

Consonant Chunks

ch	gh	ph	sh	th	wh		
gn	kn	qu	wr	dg	ck	tch	
bb	cc	dd	ff	gg	hh	kk	ll	mm
nn	pp	rr	ss	tt	vv	ww	zz

Wild Tales

Copywork

Copy the story on the lines below. Then mark the same letter patterns that you marked on the printed passage. Look at the previous page if you need help finding the chunks.

A sloth spends most of its life

A

upside down. It hangs from a

u

tree branch. The sloth digs its

t

sharp claws into the branch

s

Wild Tales **20A**

20B
Consonant Chunks

Today's Activities:

☐ Shared reading ☐ Chunking (**consonant chunks**) ☐ Copywork

A sloth spends most of its life upside down. It hangs from a tree branch. The sloth digs its sharp claws into the branch and holds on tightly. The sloth eats leaves from the tree. Then it falls asleep upside down. It is hard to get a sloth to move from its tree!

Consonant Chunks

ch	gh	ph	sh	th	wh			
gn	kn	qu	wr	dg	ck	tch		
bb	cc	dd	ff	gg	hh	kk	ll	mm
nn	pp	rr	ss	tt	vv	ww	zz	

Wild Tales

Copywork

Copy the story on the lines below. Then mark the same letter patterns that you marked on the printed passage. Look at the previous page if you need help finding the chunks.

The sloth digs its sharp claws

T

into the branch and

i

holds on tightly. The sloth

h

eats leaves from the tree.

e

Wild Tales **20B**

20C Consonant Chunks

Today's Activities:

☐ Shared reading ☐ Chunking (**consonant chunks**) ☐ Copywork

---

A sloth spends most of its life upside down. It hangs from a tree branch. The sloth digs its sharp claws into the branch and holds on tightly. The sloth eats leaves from the tree. Then it falls asleep upside down. It is hard to get a sloth to move from its tree!

Consonant Chunks

ch	gh	ph	sh	th	wh		
gn	kn	qu	wr	dg	ck	tch	
bb	cc	dd	ff	gg	hh	kk	ll	mm
nn	pp	rr	ss	tt	vv	ww	zz

Wild Tales

Copywork

Copy the story on the lines below. Then mark the same letter patterns that you marked on the printed passage. Look at the previous page if you need help finding the chunks.

The sloth eats leaves from

T

the tree. Then it falls asleep

t

upside down. It is hard to get

u

a sloth to move from its tree!

a

Wild Tales **20C**

20D Consonant Chunks

Today's Activities:

☐ Shared reading ☐ Chunking (**consonant chunks**) ☐ No Rule Day

A sloth spends most of its life upside down. It hangs from a tree branch. The sloth digs its sharp claws into the branch and holds on tightly. The sloth eats leaves from the tree. Then it falls asleep upside down. It is hard to get a sloth to move from its tree!

Consonant Chunks

ch	gh	ph	sh	th	wh		
gn	kn	qu	wr	dg	ck	tch	
bb	cc	dd	ff	gg	hh	kk	ll	mm
nn	pp	rr	ss	tt	vv	ww	zz

Wild Tales

No Rule Day

Draw a picture of the story or write your own story. Be creative and have fun.

20E Consonant Chunks

Today's Activities:

☐ Shared reading ☐ Chunking (**consonant chunks**) ☐ Dictation

---

A sloth spends most of its life upside down. It hangs from a tree branch. The sloth digs its sharp claws into the branch and holds on tightly. The sloth eats leaves from the tree. Then it falls asleep upside down. It is hard to get a sloth to move from its tree!

JAGUAR

SLOTH

CECROPIA LEAVES

A FOOD CHAIN FOR BROWN-THROATED THREE-FINGERED SLOTHS

Consonant Chunks

ch	gh	ph	sh	th	wh	
gn	kn	qu	wr	dg	ck	tch
bb	cc	dd	ff	gg	hh	kk	ll	mm
nn	pp	rr	ss	tt	vv	ww	zz

Wild Tales

Dictation

Turn the page to write this week's story from dictation.

Write this week's story from dictation. Take your time and ask for help if you need it.

A

I spelled _____ words correctly.

21A
Vowel and Consonant Chunks

See Lesson 21 in the Instructor's Handbook for instructions and tips.

Today's Activities:
☐ Shared reading ☐ Chunking (<u>vowel chunks</u>, <u>consonant chunks</u>) ☐ Copywork

What do bats eat? Some bats eat fruit or nectar from flowers. Most bats eat bugs. One bat can eat hundreds of bugs in just one night. That's a lot of bugs! Just think how many more bugs would be in the world if there were no bats!

Consonant Chunks

ch	gh	ph	sh	th	wh	
gn	kn	qu	wr	dg	ck	tch
bb	cc	dd	ff	gg	hh	kk	ll	mm
nn	pp	rr	ss	tt	vv	ww	zz

Vowel Chunks

aa	ae	ai	ao	au	aw	ay
ea	ee	ei	eo	ew	ey	eau
ia	ie	ii	io	iu		
oa	oe	oi	oo	ou	ow	oy
ua	ue	ui	uo	uy		

Wild Tales

Copywork

Copy the story on the lines below. Then mark the same letter patterns that you marked on the printed passage. Look at the previous page if you need help finding the chunks.

What do bats eat?
W

Some bats eat fruit
S

or nectar from flowers.
o

Most bats eat bugs.
M

Wild Tales **21A**

21B
Vowel and Consonant Chunks

Today's Activities:

☐ Shared reading ☐ Chunking (<u>vowel chunks</u>, <u>consonant chunks</u>) ☐ Copywork

What do bats eat? Some bats eat fruit or nectar from flowers. Most bats eat bugs. One bat can eat hundreds of bugs in just one night. That's a lot of bugs! Just think how many more bugs would be in the world if there were no bats!

Consonant Chunks

ch	gh	ph	sh	th	wh		
gn	kn	qu	wr	dg	ck	tch	
bb	cc	dd	ff	gg	hh	kk	ll	mm
nn	pp	rr	ss	tt	vv	ww	zz

Vowel Chunks

aa	ae	ai	ao	au	aw	ay
ea	ee	ei	eo	ew	ey	eau
ia	ie	ii	io	iu		
oa	oe	oi	oo	ou	ow	oy
ua	ue	ui	uo	uy		

30

Wild Tales

Copywork

Copy the story on the lines below. Then mark the same letter patterns that you marked on the printed passage. Look at the previous page if you need help finding the chunks.

Most bats eat bugs.

M

One bat can eat hundreds

O

# of bugs in just one night.

o

That's a lot of bugs!

T

Wild Tales **21B**

21C Vowel and Consonant Chunks

Today's Activities:

☐ Shared reading ☐ Chunking (<u>vowel chunks</u>, <u>consonant chunks</u>) ☐ Copywork

---

What do bats eat? Some bats eat fruit or nectar from flowers. Most bats eat bugs. One bat can eat hundreds of bugs in just one night. That's a lot of bugs! Just think how many more bugs would be in the world if there were no bats!

Consonant Chunks

ch	gh	ph	sh	th	wh		
gn	kn	qu	wr	dg	ck	tch	
bb	cc	dd	ff	gg	hh	kk	ll	mm
nn	pp	rr	ss	tt	vv	ww	zz	

Vowel Chunks

aa	ae	ai	ao	au	aw	ay
ea	ee	ei	eo	ew	ey	eau
ia	ie	ii	io	iu		
oa	oe	oi	oo	ou	ow	oy
ua	ue	ui	uo	uy		

Wild Tales

Copywork

Copy the story on the lines below. Then mark the same letter patterns that you marked on the printed passage. Look at the previous page if you need help finding the chunks.

That's a lot of bugs!

T

Just think how many more

J

bugs would be in the world

b

if there were no bats!

i

Wild Tales 21C

21D Vowel and Consonant Chunks

Today's Activities:

☐ Shared reading   ☐ Chunking (**vowel chunks**, **consonant chunks**)   ☐ No Rule Day

---

What do bats eat? Some bats eat fruit or nectar from flowers. Most bats eat bugs. One bat can eat hundreds of bugs in just one night. That's a lot of bugs! Just think how many more bugs would be in the world if there were no bats!

Consonant Chunks

ch	gh	ph	sh	th	wh		
gn	kn	qu	wr	dg	ck	tch	
bb	cc	dd	ff	gg	hh	kk	ll	mm
nn	pp	rr	ss	tt	vv	ww	zz

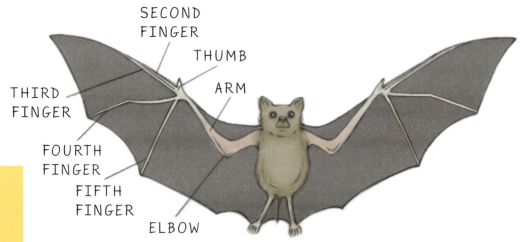

Vowel Chunks

aa	ae	ai	ao	au	aw	ay
ea	ee	ei	eo	ew	ey	eau
ia	ie	ii	io	iu		
oa	oe	oi	oo	ou	ow	oy
ua	ue	ui	uo	uy		

34   *Wild Tales*

No Rule Day

Draw a picture of the story or write your own story. Be creative and have fun.

21E
Vowel and Consonant Chunks

Today's Activities:

☐ Shared reading ☐ Chunking (<u>vowel chunks</u>, <u>consonant chunks</u>) ☐ Dictation

---

What do bats eat? Some bats eat fruit or nectar from flowers. Most bats eat bugs. One bat can eat hundreds of bugs in just one night. That's a lot of bugs! Just think how many more bugs would be in the world if there were no bats!

Consonant Chunks

ch	gh	ph	sh	th	wh		
gn	kn	qu	wr	dg	ck	tch	
bb	cc	dd	ff	gg	hh	kk	ll	mm
nn	pp	rr	ss	tt	vv	ww	zz

Vowel Chunks

aa	ae	ai	ao	au	aw	ay
ea	ee	ei	eo	ew	ey	eau
ia	ie	ii	io	iu		
oa	oe	oi	oo	ou	ow	oy
ua	ue	ui	uo	uy		

Dictation

Turn the page to write this week's story from dictation.

Wild Tales 21E

Write this week's story from dictation. Take your time and ask for help if you need it.

What

I spelled _____ words correctly.

22A Bossy *r* Chunks

📖 See Lesson 22 in the Instructor's Handbook for instructions and tips.

Today's Activities:

☐ Shared reading   ☐ Chunking (**Bossy *r* chunks**)   ☐ Copywork

A beaver's home looks like a pile of sticks in a stream. Beavers are good builders. Using their sharp teeth, they gnaw through tree branches. Then they use the branches to build a dam. The dam makes a pond. The beaver builds a house in the pond. The door to the house is under water!

Bossy r Chunks
ar er ir or ur

Copywork

Copy the story on the lines below. Then mark the same letter patterns that you marked on the printed passage. Look at the previous page if you need help finding the chunks.

A beaver's home looks

A

like a pile of sticks in a

l

stream. Beavers are good

s

builders.

b

22B
Bossy *r* Chunks

Today's Activities:

☐ Shared reading ☐ Chunking (**Bossy *r* chunks**) ☐ Copywork

---

A beaver's home looks like a pile of sticks in a stream. Beavers are good builders. Using their sharp teeth, they gnaw through tree branches. Then they use the branches to build a dam. The dam makes a pond. The beaver builds a house in the pond. The door to the house is under water!

Bossy r Chunks
ar er ir or ur

Wild Tales

Copywork

Copy the story on the lines below. Then mark the same letter patterns that you marked on the printed passage. Look at the previous page if you need help finding the chunks.

Using their sharp teeth,

U

they gnaw through tree

t

branches. Then they use the

b

branches to build a dam.

b

Wild Tales **22B**

22C
Bossy r Chunks

Today's Activities:

☐ Shared reading ☐ Chunking (**Bossy r chunks**) ☐ Copywork

A beaver's home looks like a pile of sticks in a stream. Beavers are good builders. Using their sharp teeth, they gnaw through tree branches. Then they use the branches to build a dam. The dam makes a pond. The beaver builds a house in the pond. The door to the house is under water!

Bossy r Chunks
ar   er   ir   or   ur

Wild Tales

Copywork

Copy the story on the lines below. Then mark the same letter patterns that you marked on the printed passage. Look at the previous page if you need help finding the chunks.

The dam makes a pond.

T

The beaver builds a house

T

in the pond. The door to

i

the house is under water!

t

Wild Tales 22C

22D
Bossy r Chunks

Today's Activities:

☐ Shared reading ☐ Chunking (**Bossy r chunks**) ☐ No Rule Day

---

A beaver's home looks like a pile of sticks in a stream. Beavers are good builders. Using their sharp teeth, they gnaw through tree branches. Then they use the branches to build a dam. The dam makes a pond. The beaver builds a house in the pond. The door to the house is under water!

Bossy r Chunks
ar   er   ir   or   ur

Wild Tales

No Rule Day

Draw a picture of the story or write your own story. Be creative and have fun.

22E
Bossy r Chunks

Today's Activities:

☐ Shared reading ☐ Chunking (**Bossy r chunks**) ☐ Dictation

A beaver's home looks like a pile of sticks in a stream. Beavers are good builders. Using their sharp teeth, they gnaw through tree branches. Then they use the branches to build a dam. The dam makes a pond. The beaver builds a house in the pond. The door to the house is under water!

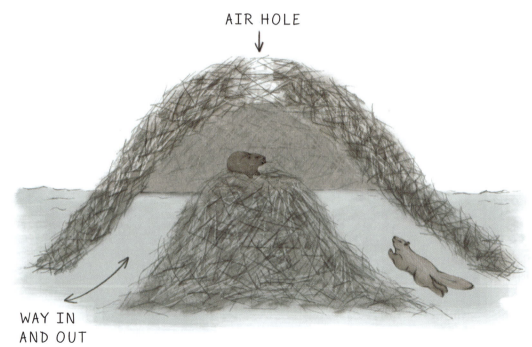

AIR HOLE

WAY IN AND OUT

NORTH AMERICAN BEAVER LODGE

Bossy r Chunks
ar   er   ir   or   ur

Dictation

Turn the page to write this week's story from dictation.

Write this week's story from dictation. Take your time and ask for help if you need it.

A

I spelled _____ words correctly.

23A
Vowel, Bossy r, and Consonant Chunks

See Lesson 23 in the Instructor's Handbook for instructions and tips.

Today's Activities:

☐ Shared reading ☐ Chunking (vowel chunks, Bossy r chunks, consonant chunks) ☐ Copywork

The king penguin does not build a nest like other birds. The mother king penguin lays just one egg. She puts the egg on top of her feet. Then she folds a flap of skin over it to keep it warm. The mother and father take turns holding the egg. One holds it while the other looks for food.

Bossy r Chunks

ar   er   ir   or   ur

Vowel Chunks

aa ae ai ao au aw ay

ea ee ei eo ew ey eau

ia ie ii io iu

oa oe oi oo ou ow oy

ua ue ui uo uy

Consonant Chunks

ch gh ph sh th wh

gn kn qu wr dg ck tch

bb cc dd ff gg hh kk ll mm

nn pp rr ss tt vv ww zz

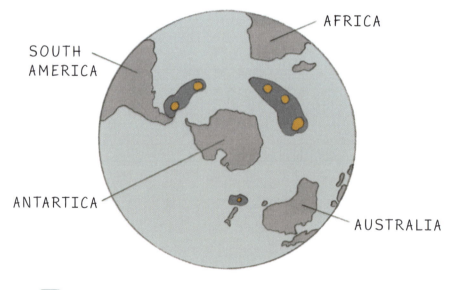

AFRICA
SOUTH AMERICA
ANTARTICA
AUSTRALIA

■ PLACES WHERE KING PENGUINS CAN BE SEEN
■ PLACES WHERE KING PENGUINS LAY EGGS

Wild Tales

Copywork

Copy the story on the lines below. Then mark the same letter patterns that you marked on the printed passage. Look at the previous page if you need help finding the chunks.

The king penguin does not

T

build a nest like other

b

birds. The mother king

b

penguin lays just one egg.

p

Wild Tales 23A

23B Vowel, Bossy r, and Consonant Chunks

Today's Activities:

☐ Shared reading ☐ Chunking (**vowel chunks**, **Bossy *r* chunks**, **consonant chunks**) ☐ Copywork

The king penguin does not build a nest like other birds. The mother king penguin lays just one egg. She puts the egg on top of her feet. Then she folds a flap of skin over it to keep it warm. The mother and father take turns holding the egg. One holds it while the other looks for food.

Bossy r Chunks
ar   er   ir   or   ur

Vowel Chunks

aa	ae	ai	ao	au	aw	ay
ea	ee	ei	eo	ew	ey	eau
ia	ie	ii	io	iu		
oa	oe	oi	oo	ou	ow	oy
ua	ue	ui	uo	uy		

Consonant Chunks

ch	gh	ph	sh	th	wh		
gn	kn	qu	wr	dg	ck	tch	
bb	cc	dd	ff	gg	hh	kk	ll	mm
nn	pp	rr	ss	tt	vv	ww	zz

Wild Tales

Copywork

Copy the story on the lines below. Then mark the same letter patterns that you marked on the printed passage. Look at the previous page if you need help finding the chunks.

She puts the egg on top

of her feet. Then she folds

a flap of skin over it

to keep it warm.

23C Vowel, Bossy r, and Consonant Chunks

Today's Activities:

☐ Shared reading   ☐ Chunking (<u>vowel chunks</u>, <u>Bossy *r* chunks</u>, <u>consonant chunks</u>)   ☐ Copywork

---

The king penguin does not build a nest like other birds. The mother king penguin lays just one egg. She puts the egg on top of her feet. Then she folds a flap of skin over it to keep it warm. The mother and father take turns holding the egg. One holds it while the other looks for food.

Bossy r Chunks

ar   er   ir   or   ur

Vowel Chunks

aa   ae   ai   ao   au   aw   ay

ea   ee   ei   eo   ew   ey   eau

ia   ie   ii   io   iu

oa   oe   oi   oo   ou   ow   oy

ua   ue   ui   uo   uy

Consonant Chunks

ch   gh   ph   sh   th   wh

gn   kn   qu   wr   dg   ck   tch

bb   cc   dd   ff   gg   hh   kk   ll   mm

nn   pp   rr   ss   tt   vv   ww   zz

Wild Tales

Copywork

Copy the story on the lines below. Then mark the same letter patterns that you marked on the printed passage. Look at the previous page if you need help finding the chunks.

The mother and father take

turns holding the egg.

One holds it while the

other looks for food.

23D Vowel, Bossy r, and Consonant Chunks

Today's Activities:

☐ Shared reading   ☐ Chunking (**vowel chunks**, **Bossy *r* chunks**, **consonant chunks**)   ☐ No Rule Day

The king penguin does not build a nest like other birds. The mother king penguin lays just one egg. She puts the egg on top of her feet. Then she folds a flap of skin over it to keep it warm. The mother and father take turns holding the egg. One holds it while the other looks for food.

Bossy r Chunks

ar er ir or ur

Vowel Chunks

aa ae ai ao au aw ay

ea ee ei eo ew ey eau

ia ie ii io iu

oa oe oi oo ou ow oy

ua ue ui uo uy

Consonant Chunks

ch gh ph sh th wh

gn kn qu wr dg ck tch

bb cc dd ff gg hh kk ll mm

nn pp rr ss tt vv ww zz

Wild Tales

No Rule Day

Draw a picture of the story or write your own story. Be creative and have fun.

23E Vowel, Bossy r, and Consonant Chunks

Today's Activities:

☐ Shared reading   ☐ Chunking (**vowel chunks**, **Bossy *r* chunks**, **consonant chunks**)   ☐ Dictation

The king penguin does not build a nest like other birds. The mother king penguin lays just one egg. She puts the egg on top of her feet. Then she folds a flap of skin over it to keep it warm. The mother and father take turns holding the egg. One holds it while the other looks for food.

Bossy r Chunks
ar   er   ir   or   ur

Vowel Chunks

aa	ae	ai	ao	au	aw	ay
ea	ee	ei	eo	ew	ey	eau
ia	ie	ii	io	iu		
oa	oe	oi	oo	ou	ow	oy
ua	ue	ui	uo	uy		

Consonant Chunks

ch	gh	ph	sh	th	wh	
gn	kn	qu	wr	dg	ck	tch
bb	cc	dd	ff	gg	hh	kk	ll	mm
nn	pp	rr	ss	tt	vv	ww	zz	

Wild Tales

Dictation

Turn the page to write this week's story from dictation.

Write this week's story from dictation. Take your time and ask for help if you need it.

The

I spelled _____ words correctly.

24A
Vowel, Bossy r, and Consonant Chunks

📖 See Lesson 24 in the Instructor's Handbook for instructions and tips.

Today's Activities:

☐ Shared reading ☐ Chunking (<u>vowel chunks</u>, <u>Bossy r chunks</u>, <u>consonant chunks</u>) ☐ Copywork

Most people know a raccoon by its mask. Raccoons also have paws that look like hands. They use their paws for climbing and catching food. They can even pull lids off trash cans! A raccoon's paws are very handy.

Consonant Chunks

ch	gh	ph	sh	th	wh	
gn	kn	qu	wr	dg	ck	tch
bb	cc	dd	ff	gg	hh	kk	ll	mm
nn	pp	rr	ss	tt	vv	ww	zz

Bossy r Chunks

ar er ir or ur

Vowel Chunks

aa	ae	ai	ao	au	aw	ay
ea	ee	ei	eo	ew	ey	eau
ia	ie	ii	io	iu		
oa	oe	oi	oo	ou	ow	oy
ua	ue	ui	uo	uy		

64

Wild Tales

Copywork

Copy the story on the lines below. Then mark the same letter patterns that you marked on the printed passage. Look at the previous page if you need help finding the chunks.

Most people know a raccoon

M

by its mask. Raccoons also have

b

paws that look like hands. They

P

use their paws for climbing

u

24B
Vowel, Bossy r, and Consonant Chunks

Today's Activities:

☐ Shared reading ☐ Chunking (<u>vowel chunks</u>, <u>**Bossy *r* chunks**</u>, <u>**consonant chunks**</u>) ☐ Copywork

Most people know a raccoon by its mask. Raccoons also have paws that look like hands. They use their paws for climbing and catching food. They can even pull lids off trash cans! A raccoon's paws are very handy.

Consonant Chunks

ch	gh	ph	sh	th	wh	
gn	kn	qu	wr	dg	ck	tch
bb	cc	dd	ff	gg	hh	kk	ll	mm
nn	pp	rr	ss	tt	vv	ww	zz

Bossy r Chunks

ar er ir or ur

Vowel Chunks

aa	ae	ai	ao	au	aw	ay
ea	ee	ei	eo	ew	ey	eau
ia	ie	ii	io	iu		
oa	oe	oi	oo	ou	ow	oy
ua	ue	ui	uo	uy		

Wild Tales

Copywork

Copy the story on the lines below. Then mark the same letter patterns that you marked on the printed passage. Look at the previous page if you need help finding the chunks.

They use their paws for

climbing and catching food.

They can even pull lids off

trash cans!

Wild Tales **24B**

24C
Vowel, Bossy *r*, and Consonant Chunks

Today's Activities:

☐ Shared reading ☐ Chunking (<u>vowel chunks</u>, <u>Bossy *r* chunks</u>, <u>consonant chunks</u>) ☐ Copywork

Most people know a raccoon by its mask. Raccoons also have paws that look like hands. They use their paws for climbing and catching food. They can even pull lids off trash cans! A raccoon's paws are very handy.

Bossy r Chunks
ar   er   ir   or   ur

Consonant Chunks
ch	gh	ph	sh	th	wh	
gn	kn	qu	wr	dg	ck	tch
bb	cc	dd	ff	gg	hh	kk	ll	mm
nn	pp	rr	ss	tt	vv	ww	zz

Vowel Chunks
aa	ae	ai	ao	au	aw	ay
ea	ee	ei	eo	ew	ey	eau
ia	ie	ii	io	iu		
oa	oe	oi	oo	ou	ow	oy
ua	ue	ui	uo	uy		

Wild Tales

Copywork

Copy the story on the lines below. Then mark the same letter patterns that you marked on the printed passage. Look at the previous page if you need help finding the chunks.

Most people know a raccoon

by its mask. Raccoons also have

paws that look like hands. They

use their paws for climbing

Wild Tales 24C

24D Vowel, Bossy r, and Consonant Chunks

Today's Activities:

☐ Shared reading   ☐ Chunking (**vowel chunks**, **Bossy r chunks**, **consonant chunks**)   ☐ No Rule Day

Most people know a raccoon by its mask. Raccoons also have paws that look like hands. They use their paws for climbing and catching food. They can even pull lids off trash cans! A raccoon's paws are very handy.

Bossy r Chunks

ar   er   ir   or   ur

Consonant Chunks

ch	gh	ph	sh	th	wh	
gn	kn	qu	wr	dg	ck	tch
bb	cc	dd	ff	gg	hh	kk	ll	mm
nn	pp	rr	ss	tt	vv	ww	zz

Vowel Chunks

aa	ae	ai	ao	au	aw	ay
ea	ee	ei	eo	ew	ey	eau
ia	ie	ii	io	iu		
oa	oe	oi	oo	ou	ow	oy
ua	ue	ui	uo	uy		

Wild Tales

No Rule Day

Draw a picture of the story or write your own story. Be creative and have fun.

24E

Vowel, Bossy *r*, and Consonant Chunks

Today's Activities:

☐ Shared reading ☐ Chunking (**vowel chunks**, **Bossy *r* chunks**, **consonant chunks**) ☐ Dictation

Most people know a raccoon by its mask. Raccoons also have paws that look like hands. They use their paws for climbing and catching food. They can even pull lids off trash cans! A raccoon's paws are very handy.

Consonant Chunks

ch	gh	ph	sh	th	wh		
gn	kn	qu	wr	dg	ck	tch	
bb	cc	dd	ff	gg	hh	kk	ll	mm
nn	pp	rr	ss	tt	vv	ww	zz

Bossy r Chunks

ar er ir or ur

Vowel Chunks

aa	ae	ai	ao	au	aw	ay
ea	ee	ei	eo	ew	ey	eau
ia	ie	ii	io	iu		
oa	oe	oi	oo	ou	ow	oy
ua	ue	ui	uo	uy		

Wild Tales

Dictation

Turn the page to write this week's story from dictation.

Wild Tales **24E**

Write this week's story from dictation. Take your time and ask for help if you need it.

Most

I spelled _____ words correctly.

25A
Vowel, Bossy r, and Consonant Chunks; Silent Letters

See Lesson 25 in the Instructor's Handbook for instructions and tips.

Today's Activities:

☐ Shared reading ☐ Chunking (<u>vowel chunks</u>, <u>Bossy *r* chunks</u>, <u>consonant chunks</u>, <u>silent letters</u>) ☐ Copywork

---

A porcupine's quills lie flat until it is scared. Then they stand straight up! If something touches a porcupine, quills come loose. A quill slides easily into an enemy's skin. On the tip of the quill are rows of tiny, sharp hooks. They hold the quill in when it is pulled. Ouch!

Vowel Chunks

aa	ae	ai	ao	au	aw	ay
ea	ee	ei	eo	ew	ey	eau
ia	ie	ii	io	iu		
oa	oe	oi	oo	ou	ow	oy
ua	ue	ui	uo	uy		

Bossy r Chunks

ar er ir or ur

Consonant Chunks

ch	gh	ph	sh	th	wh		
gn	kn	qu	wr	dg	ck	tch	
bb	cc	dd	ff	gg	hh	kk	ll	mm
nn	pp	rr	ss	tt	vv	ww	zz

Wild Tales

Copywork

Copy the story on the lines below. Then mark the same letter patterns that you marked on the printed passage. Look at the previous page if you need help finding the chunks.

A porcupine's quills lie

A

flat until it is scared.

f

Then they stand straight up!

T

If something touches

I

25B
Vowel, Bossy r, and Consonant Chunks; Silent Letters

Today's Activities:

☐ Shared reading ☐ Chunking (<u>vowel chunks</u>, <u>Bossy *r* chunks</u>, <u>consonant chunks</u>, <u>silent letters</u>) ☐ Copywork

---

A porcupine's quills lie flat until it is scared. Then they stand straight up! If something touches a porcupine, quills come loose. A quill slides easily into an enemy's skin. On the tip of the quill are rows of tiny, sharp hooks. They hold the quill in when it is pulled. Ouch!

Vowel Chunks

aa	ae	ai	ao	au	aw	ay
ea	ee	ei	eo	ew	ey	eau
ia	ie	ii	io	iu		
oa	oe	oi	oo	ou	ow	oy
ua	ue	ui	uo	uy		

Bossy r Chunks

ar er ir or ur

Consonant Chunks

ch	gh	ph	sh	th	wh	
gn	kn	qu	wr	dg	ck	tch
bb	cc	dd	ff	gg	hh	kk	ll	mm
nn	pp	rr	ss	tt	vv	ww	zz

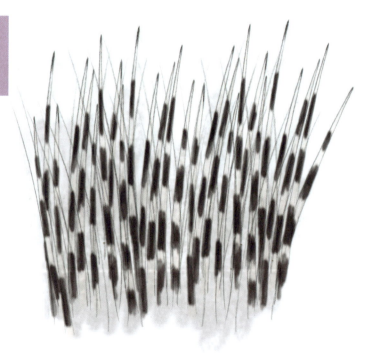

Wild Tales

Copywork

Copy the story on the lines below. Then mark the same letter patterns that you marked on the printed passage. Look at the previous page if you need help finding the chunks.

If something touches a

porcupine, quills come loose.

A quill slides easily

into an enemy's skin.

25C Vowel, Bossy r, and Consonant Chunks; Silent Letters

Today's Activities:

☐ Shared reading ☐ Chunking (<u>vowel chunks</u>, <u>Bossy *r* chunks</u>, <u>consonant chunks</u>, <u>silent letters</u>) ☐ Copywork

---

A porcupine's quills lie flat until it is scared. Then they stand straight up! If something touches a porcupine, quills come loose. A quill slides easily into an enemy's skin. On the tip of the quill are rows of tiny, sharp hooks. They hold the quill in when it is pulled. Ouch!

Vowel Chunks

aa	ae	ai	ao	au	aw	ay
ea	ee	ei	eo	ew	ey	eau
ia	ie	ii	io	iu		
oa	oe	oi	oo	ou	ow	oy
ua	ue	ui	uo	uy		

Bossy r Chunks

ar er ir or ur

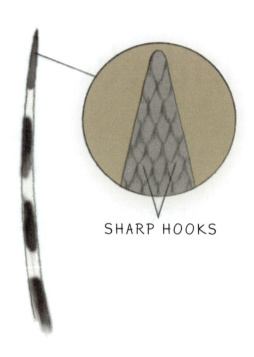

SHARP HOOKS

Consonant Chunks

ch	gh	ph	sh	th	wh	
gn	kn	qu	wr	dg	ck	tch
bb	cc	dd	ff	gg	hh	kk	ll	mm
nn	pp	rr	ss	tt	vv	ww	zz

Wild Tales

Copywork

Copy the story on the lines below. Then mark the same letter patterns that you marked on the printed passage. Look at the previous page if you need help finding the chunks.

On the tip of a quill

are rows of tiny, sharp hooks.

They hold the quill in

when it is pulled. Ouch!

25D
Vowel, Bossy *r*, and Consonant Chunks; Silent Letters

Today's Activities:

☐ Shared reading ☐ Chunking (**vowel chunks**, **Bossy *r* chunks**, **consonant chunks**, **silent letters**) ☐ No Rule Day

---

A porcupine's quills lie flat until it is scared. Then they stand straight up! If something touches a porcupine, quills come loose. A quill slides easily into an enemy's skin. On the tip of the quill are rows of tiny, sharp hooks. They hold the quill in when it is pulled. Ouch!

Vowel Chunks

aa	ae	ai	ao	au	aw	ay
ea	ee	ei	eo	ew	ey	eau
ia	ie	ii	io	iu		
oa	oe	oi	oo	ou	ow	oy
ua	ue	ui	uo	uy		

Bossy r Chunks

ar er ir or ur

Consonant Chunks

ch	gh	ph	sh	th	wh	
gn	kn	qu	wr	dg	ck	tch
bb	cc	dd	ff	gg	hh	kk	ll	mm
nn	pp	rr	ss	tt	vv	ww	zz

Wild Tales

No Rule Day

Draw a picture of the story or write your own story. Be creative and have fun.

25E Vowel, Bossy r, and Consonant Chunks; Silent Letters

Today's Activities:

☐ Shared reading ☐ Chunking (**vowel chunks**, **Bossy r chunks**, **consonant chunks**, **silent letters**) ☐ Dictation

---

A porcupine's quills lie flat until it is scared. Then they stand straight up! If something touches a porcupine, quills come loose. A quill slides easily into an enemy's skin. On the tip of the quill are rows of tiny, sharp hooks. They hold the quill in when it is pulled. Ouch!

Vowel Chunks

aa	ae	ai	ao	au	aw	ay
ea	ee	ei	eo	ew	ey	eau
ia	ie	ii	io	iu		
oa	oe	oi	oo	ou	ow	oy
ua	ue	ui	uo	uy		

Bossy r Chunks

ar   er   ir   or   ur

Consonant Chunks

ch	gh	ph	sh	th	wh	
gn	kn	qu	wr	dg	ck	tch
bb	cc	dd	ff	gg	hh	kk	ll	mm
nn	pp	rr	ss	tt	vv	ww	zz	

Wild Tales

Dictation

Turn the page to write this week's story from dictation.

Write this week's story from dictation. Take your time and ask for help if you need it.

A

I spelled _____ words correctly.

26A
Vowel, Bossy *r*, and Consonant Chunks; Silent Letters

See Lesson 26 in the Instructor's Handbook for instructions and tips.

Today's Activities:

☐ Shared reading ☐ Chunking (<u>vowel chunks</u>, <u>Bossy *r* chunks</u>, <u>consonant chunks</u>, <u>silent letters</u>) ☐ Copywork

A great white shark has a huge mouth. It is filled with rows of teeth. When a shark has lost one tooth, another tooth will move up to fill the empty space. A shark will have thousands of teeth over its lifetime.

Vowel Chunks

aa	ae	ai	ao	au	aw	ay
ea	ee	ei	eo	ew	ey	eau
ia	ie	ii	io	iu		
oa	oe	oi	oo	ou	ow	oy
ua	ue	ui	uo	uy		

Bossy r Chunks

ar er ir or ur

Consonant Chunks

ch	gh	ph	sh	th	wh		
gn	kn	qu	wr	dg	ck	tch	
bb	cc	dd	ff	gg	hh	kk	ll	mm
nn	pp	rr	ss	tt	vv	ww	zz

88

Wild Tales

Copywork

Copy the story on the lines below. Then mark the same letter patterns that you marked on the printed passage. Look at the previous page if you need help finding the chunks.

A great white shark has

A

a huge mouth. It is filled

a

with rows of teeth. When a

W

shark has lost one tooth,

s

Wild Tales 26A

26B
Vowel, Bossy *r*, and Consonant Chunks; Silent Letters

Today's Activities:

☐ Shared reading   ☐ Chunking (**vowel chunks**, **Bossy *r* chunks**, **consonant chunks**, **silent letters**)   ☐ Copywork

---

A great white shark has a huge mouth. It is filled with rows of teeth. When a shark has lost one tooth, another tooth will move up to fill the empty space. A shark will have thousands of teeth over its lifetime.

Vowel Chunks

aa	ae	ai	ao	au	aw	ay
ea	ee	ei	eo	ew	ey	eau
ia	ie	ii	io	iu		
oa	oe	oi	oo	ou	ow	oy
ua	ue	ui	uo	uy		

Bossy r Chunks

ar   er   ir   or   ur

Consonant Chunks

ch	gh	ph	sh	th	wh		
gn	kn	qu	wr	dg	ck	tch	
bb	cc	dd	ff	gg	hh	kk	ll	mm
nn	pp	rr	ss	tt	vv	ww	zz

Wild Tales

Copywork

Copy the story on the lines below. Then mark the same letter patterns that you marked on the printed passage. Look at the previous page if you need help finding the chunks.

When a shark has lost

W

one tooth, another tooth

o

will move up to fill

w

the empty space.

t

26C
Vowel, Bossy *r*, and Consonant Chunks; Silent Letters

Today's Activities:

☐ Shared reading ☐ Chunking (<u>vowel chunks</u>, <u>Bossy *r* chunks</u>, <u>consonant chunks</u>, <u>silent letters</u>) ☐ Copywork

A great white shark has a huge mouth. It is filled with rows of teeth. When a shark has lost one tooth, another tooth will move up to fill the empty space. A shark will have thousands of teeth over its lifetime.

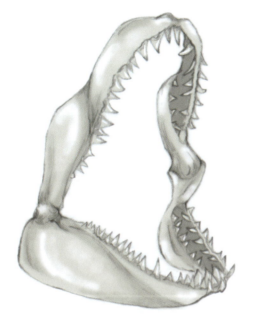

ROWS OF TEETH IN A GREAT WHITE SHARK JAW

Vowel Chunks

aa	ae	ai	ao	au	aw	ay
ea	ee	ei	eo	ew	ey	eau
ia	ie	ii	io	iu		
oa	oe	oi	oo	ou	ow	oy
ua	ue	ui	uo	uy		

Bossy r Chunks

ar	er	ir	or	ur

Consonant Chunks

ch	gh	ph	sh	th	wh	
gn	kn	qu	wr	dg	ck	tch
bb	cc	dd	ff	gg	hh	kk	ll	mm
nn	pp	rr	ss	tt	vv	ww	zz	

Wild Tales

Copywork

Copy the story on the lines below. Then mark the same letter patterns that you marked on the printed passage. Look at the previous page if you need help finding the chunks.

another tooth will move up

a

to fill the empty space.

t

A shark will have thousands

A

of teeth over its lifetime.

o

Wild Tales 26C

26D
Vowel, Bossy r, and Consonant Chunks; Silent Letters

Today's Activities:

☐ Shared reading ☐ Chunking (vowel chunks, Bossy *r* chunks, consonant chunks, silent letters) ☐ No Rule Day

A great white shark has a huge mouth. It is filled with rows of teeth. When a shark has lost one tooth, another tooth will move up to fill the empty space. A shark will have thousands of teeth over its lifetime.

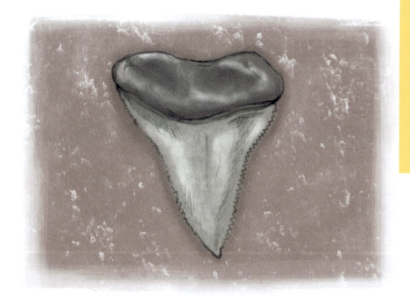

Vowel Chunks

aa	ae	ai	ao	au	aw	ay
ea	ee	ei	eo	ew	ey	eau
ia	ie	ii	io	iu		
oa	oe	oi	oo	ou	ow	oy
ua	ue	ui	uo	uy		

Bossy r Chunks

ar er ir or ur

Consonant Chunks

ch	gh	ph	sh	th	wh		
gn	kn	qu	wr	dg	ck	tch	
bb	cc	dd	ff	gg	hh	kk	ll	mm
nn	pp	rr	ss	tt	vv	ww	zz	

Wild Tales

No Rule Day

Draw a picture of the story or write your own story. Be creative and have fun.

26E

Vowel, Bossy *r*, and Consonant Chunks; Silent Letters

Today's Activities:

☐ Shared reading ☐ Chunking (vowel chunks, Bossy *r* chunks, consonant chunks, silent letters) ☐ Dictation

A great white shark has a huge mouth. It is filled with rows of teeth. When a shark has lost one tooth, another tooth will move up to fill the empty space. A shark will have thousands of teeth over its lifetime.

Vowel Chunks

aa	ae	ai	ao	au	aw	ay
ea	ee	ei	eo	ew	ey	eau
ia	ie	ii	io	iu		
oa	oe	oi	oo	ou	ow	oy
ua	ue	ui	uo	uy		

Bossy r Chunks

ar er ir or ur

Consonant Chunks

ch	gh	ph	sh	th	wh	
gn	kn	qu	wr	dg	ck	tch
bb	cc	dd	ff	gg	hh	kk	ll	mm
nn	pp	rr	ss	tt	vv	ww	zz	

96

Wild Tales

Dictation

Turn the page to write this week's story from dictation.

Write this week's story from dictation. Take your time and ask for help if you need it.

A

I spelled _____ words correctly.

27A
Vowel, Bossy r, and Consonant Chunks; Endings, Silent Letters

See Lesson 27 in the Instructor's Handbook for instructions and tips.

Today's Activities:

☐ Shared reading ☐ Chunking (vowel chunks, Bossy r chunks, consonant chunks, endings, silent letters) ☐ Copywork

---

Jellyfish are not really fish. The jellyfish looks like an umbrella. Long tentacles hang down. Be careful! Tentacles give a shock! Jellyfish use their tentacles for catching food and fighting enemies.

Consonant Chunks

ch	gh	ph	sh	th	wh
gn	kn	qu	wr	dg	ck	tch
bb	cc	dd	ff	gg	hh	kk	ll	mm
nn	pp	rr	ss	tt	vv	ww	zz

Vowel Chunks

aa	ae	ai	ao	au	aw	ay
ea	ee	ei	eo	ew	ey	eau
ia	ie	ii	io	iu		
oa	oe	oi	oo	ou	ow	oy
ua	ue	ui	uo	uy		

Endings

-ed   -es   -ful   -ing   -ly

Bossy r Chunks

ar   er   ir   or   ur

Wild Tales

Copywork

Copy the story on the lines below. Then mark the same letter patterns that you marked on the printed passage. Look at the previous page if you need help finding the chunks.

Jellyfish are not really fish.

J

The jellyfish looks like

T

an umbrella. Long tentacles

a

hang down. Be careful!

h

27B
Vowel, Bossy r, and Consonant Chunks; Endings, Silent Letters

Today's Activities:

☐ Shared reading ☐ Chunking (<u>vowel chunks</u>, <u>Bossy r chunks</u>, <u>consonant chunks</u>, <u>endings</u>, <u>silent letters</u>) ☐ Copywork

Jellyfish are not really fish. The jellyfish looks like an umbrella. Long tentacles hang down. Be careful! Tentacles give a shock! Jellyfish use their tentacles for catching food and fighting enemies.

Consonant Chunks

ch	gh	ph	sh	th	wh		
gn	kn	qu	wr	dg	ck	tch	
bb	cc	dd	ff	gg	hh	kk	ll	mm
nn	pp	rr	ss	tt	vv	ww	zz

Vowel Chunks

aa	ae	ai	ao	au	aw	ay
ea	ee	ei	eo	ew	ey	eau
ia	ie	ii	io	iu
oa	oe	oi	oo	ou	ow	oy
ua	ue	ui	uo	uy

Endings

-ed -es -ful -ing -ly

Bossy r Chunks

ar er ir or ur

Wild Tales

Copywork

Copy the story on the lines below. Then mark the same letter patterns that you marked on the printed passage. Look at the previous page if you need help finding the chunks.

Be careful! Tentacles give

a shock! Jellyfish use their

tentacles for catching food

and fighting enemies.

27C

Vowel, Bossy r, and Consonant Chunks; Endings, Silent Letters

Today's Activities:

☐ Shared reading ☐ Chunking (<u>vowel chunks</u>, <u>Bossy *r* chunks</u>, <u>consonant chunks</u>, <u>endings</u>, <u>silent letters</u>) ☐ Copywork

Jellyfish are not really fish. The jellyfish looks like an umbrella. Long tentacles hang down. Be careful! Tentacles give a shock! Jellyfish use their tentacles for catching food and fighting enemies.

Consonant Chunks

ch	gh	ph	sh	th	wh	
gn	kn	qu	wr	dg	ck	tch
bb	cc	dd	ff	gg	hh	kk	ll	mm
nn	pp	rr	ss	tt	vv	ww	zz

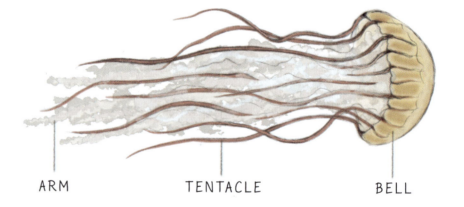

ARM   TENTACLE   BELL

Vowel Chunks

aa	ae	ai	ao	au	aw	ay
ea	ee	ei	eo	ew	ey	eau
ia	ie	ii	io	iu		
oa	oe	oi	oo	ou	ow	oy
ua	ue	ui	uo	uy		

Endings

-ed -es -ful -ing -ly

Bossy r Chunks

ar   er   ir   or   ur

Wild Tales

Copywork

Copy the story on the lines below. Then mark the same letter patterns that you marked on the printed passage. Look at the previous page if you need help finding the chunks.

Jellyfish are not really fish.

The jellyfish looks like

an umbrella. Long tentacles

hang down. Be careful!

Wild Tales 27C

27D
Vowel, Bossy r, and Consonant Chunks; Endings, Silent Letters

Today's Activities:

☐ Shared reading ☐ Chunking (<u>vowel chunks</u>, <u>Bossy r chunks</u>, <u>consonant chunks</u>, <u>endings</u>, <u>silent letters</u>) ☐ No Rule Day

Jellyfish are not really fish. The jellyfish looks like an umbrella. Long tentacles hang down. Be careful! Tentacles give a shock! Jellyfish use their tentacles for catching food and fighting enemies.

Consonant Chunks

ch	gh	ph	sh	th	wh
gn	kn	qu	wr	dg	ck	tch
bb	cc	dd	ff	gg	hh	kk	ll	mm
nn	pp	rr	ss	tt	vv	ww	zz

Vowel Chunks

aa ae ai ao au aw ay
ea ee ei eo ew ey eau
ia ie ii io iu
oa oe oi oo ou ow oy
ua ue ui uo uy

Endings

-ed -es -ful -ing -ly

Bossy r Chunks

ar er ir or ur

Wild Tales

No Rule Day

Draw a picture of the story or write your own story. Be creative and have fun.

27E

Vowel, Bossy r, and Consonant Chunks; Endings, Silent Letters

Today's Activities:

☐ Shared reading   ☐ Chunking (vowel chunks, Bossy *r* chunks, consonant chunks, endings, silent letters)   ☐ Dictation

Jellyfish are not really fish. The jellyfish looks like an umbrella. Long tentacles hang down. Be careful! Tentacles give a shock! Jellyfish use their tentacles for catching food and fighting enemies.

Consonant Chunks

ch	gh	ph	sh	th	wh	
gn	kn	qu	wr	dg	ck	tch
bb	cc	dd	ff	gg	hh	kk	ll	mm
nn	pp	rr	ss	tt	vv	ww	zz

Vowel Chunks

aa	ae	ai	ao	au	aw	ay
ea	ee	ei	eo	ew	ey	eau
ia	ie	ii	io	iu		
oa	oe	oi	oo	ou	ow	oy
ua	ue	ui	uo	uy		

Endings

-ed -es -ful -ing -ly

Bossy r Chunks

ar   er   ir   or   ur

Wild Tales

Dictation

Turn the page to write this week's story from dictation.

Write this week's story from dictation. Take your time and ask for help if you need it.

Jellyfish

I spelled _____ words correctly.

28A
Vowel, Bossy *r*, and Consonant Chunks; Tricky *y* Guy

📖 See Lesson 28 in the Instructor's Handbook for instructions and tips.

Today's Activities:

☐ Shared reading   ☐ Chunking (**vowel chunks**, **Bossy *r* chunks**, **consonant chunks**, **Tricky *y* Guy**)   ☐ Copywork

---

When it is hot, do you play in water to cool off? Some kangaroos have a funny way of getting cool. They lick their furry arms until they are wet. Then the air dries their fur. As the fur becomes dry, the kangaroo cools off.

Vowel Chunks

aa	ae	ai	ao	au	aw	ay
ea	ee	ei	eo	ew	ey	eau
ia	ie	ii	io	iu		
oa	oe	oi	oo	ou	ow	oy
ua	ue	ui	uo	uy		

Bossy r Chunks

ar er ir or ur

Consonant Chunks

ch	gh	ph	sh	th	wh		
gn	kn	qu	wr	dg	ck	tch	
bb	cc	dd	ff	gg	hh	kk	ll	mm
nn	pp	rr	ss	tt	vv	ww	zz	

112

Wild Tales

Copywork

Copy the story on the lines below. Then mark the same letter patterns that you marked on the printed passage. Look at the previous page if you need help finding the chunks.

When it is hot, do you

play in water to cool off?

Some kangaroos have a

funny way of getting cool.

Wild Tales **28A**

28B
Vowel, Bossy r, and Consonant Chunks; Tricky y Guy

Today's Activities:

☐ Shared reading ☐ Chunking (<u>vowel chunks</u>, <u>Bossy *r* chunks</u>, <u>consonant chunks</u>, <u>Tricky *y* Guy</u>) ☐ Copywork

When it is hot, do you play in water to cool off? Some kangaroos have a funny way of getting cool. They lick their furry arms until they are wet. Then the air dries their fur. As the fur becomes dry, the kangaroo cools off.

Vowel Chunks

aa	ae	ai	ao	au	aw	ay
ea	ee	ei	eo	ew	ey	eau
ia	ie	ii	io	iu		
oa	oe	oi	oo	ou	ow	oy
ua	ue	ui	uo	uy		

Bossy r Chunks

ar er ir or ur

Consonant Chunks

ch	gh	ph	sh	th	wh		
gn	kn	qu	wr	dg	ck	tch	
bb	cc	dd	ff	gg	hh	kk	ll	mm
nn	pp	rr	ss	tt	vv	ww	zz	

Wild Tales

Copywork

Copy the story on the lines below. Then mark the same letter patterns that you marked on the printed passage. Look at the previous page if you need help finding the chunks.

They lick their furry arms until

they are wet. Then the air dries

their fur. As the fur becomes

dry, the kangaroo cools off.

28C
Vowel, Bossy r, and Consonant Chunks; Tricky y Guy

Today's Activities:

☐ Shared reading ☐ Chunking (**vowel chunks**, **Bossy r chunks**, **consonant chunks**, **Tricky y Guy**) ☐ Copywork

---

When it is hot, do you play in water to cool off? Some kangaroos have a funny way of getting cool. They lick their furry arms until they are wet. Then the air dries their fur. As the fur becomes dry, the kangaroo cools off.

Vowel Chunks

aa	ae	ai	ao	au	aw	ay
ea	ee	ei	eo	ew	ey	eau
ia	ie	ii	io	iu		
oa	oe	oi	oo	ou	ow	oy
ua	ue	ui	uo	uy		

Bossy r Chunks

ar er ir or ur

Consonant Chunks

ch	gh	ph	sh	th	wh	
gn	kn	qu	wr	dg	ck	tch
bb	cc	dd	ff	gg	hh	kk	ll	mm
nn	pp	rr	ss	tt	vv	ww	zz	

116

Wild Tales

Copywork

Copy the story on the lines below. Then mark the same letter patterns that you marked on the printed passage. Look at the previous page if you need help finding the chunks.

When it is hot, do you

play in water to cool off?

Some kangaroos have a

funny way of getting cool.

Wild Tales 28C

28D

Vowel, Bossy *r*, and Consonant Chunks; Tricky *y* Guy

Today's Activities:

☐ Shared reading   ☐ Chunking (<u>vowel chunks</u>, <u>Bossy *r* chunks</u>, <u>consonant chunks</u>, <u>Tricky *y* Guy</u>)   ☐ No Rule Day

When it is hot, do you play in water to cool off? Some kangaroos have a funny way of getting cool. They lick their furry arms until they are wet. Then the air dries their fur. As the fur becomes dry, the kangaroo cools off.

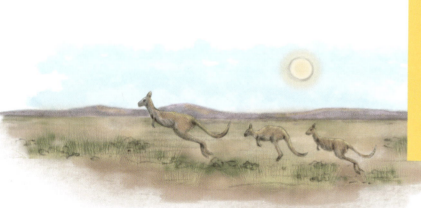

Vowel Chunks

aa	ae	ai	ao	au	aw	ay
ea	ee	ei	eo	ew	ey	eau
ia	ie	ii	io	iu		
oa	oe	oi	oo	ou	ow	oy
ua	ue	ui	uo	uy		

Bossy r Chunks

ar   er   ir   or   ur

Consonant Chunks

ch	gh	ph	sh	th	wh	
gn	kn	qu	wr	dg	ck	tch
bb	cc	dd	ff	gg	hh	kk	ll	mm
nn	pp	rr	ss	tt	vv	ww	zz	

Wild Tales

No Rule Day

Draw a picture of the story or write your own story. Be creative and have fun.

28E

Vowel, Bossy r, and Consonant Chunks; Tricky y Guy

Today's Activities:

☐ Shared reading ☐ Chunking (**vowel chunks**, **Bossy r chunks**, **consonant chunks**, **Tricky y Guy**) ☐ Dictation

---

When it is hot, do you play in water to cool off? Some kangaroos have a funny way of getting cool. They lick their furry arms until they are wet. Then the air dries their fur. As the fur becomes dry, the kangaroo cools off.

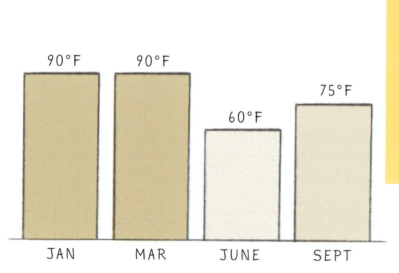

AVERAGE TEMPERATURES OF A PLACE WHERE RED KANGAROOS LIVE

Vowel Chunks

aa	ae	ai	ao	au	aw	ay
ea	ee	ei	eo	ew	ey	eau
ia	ie	ii	io	iu		
oa	oe	oi	oo	ou	ow	oy
ua	ue	ui	uo	uy		

Bossy r Chunks

ar er ir or ur

Consonant Chunks

ch	gh	ph	sh	th	wh	
gn	kn	qu	wr	dg	ck	tch
bb	cc	dd	ff	gg	hh	kk	ll	mm
nn	pp	rr	ss	tt	vv	ww	zz

120

Wild Tales

Dictation

Turn the page to write this week's story from dictation.

Write this week's story from dictation. Take your time and ask for help if you need it.

When

I spelled _____ words correctly.

29A

Vowel, Bossy *r*, and Consonant Chunks; Endings, Silent Letters

See Lesson 29 in the Instructor's Handbook for instructions and tips.

Today's Activities:

☐ Shared reading ☐ Chunking (vowel chunks, Bossy *r* chunks, consonant chunks, endings, silent letters) ☐ Copywork

---

Can you guess how howler monkeys got their name? They howl in the morning and in the evening. People can hear the howls up to three miles away. Some people think the males are the loudest animals on land.

Endings
-ed -es -ful -ing -ly

Bossy r Chunks
ar er ir or ur

Consonant Chunks
ch gh ph sh th wh
gn kn qu wr dg ck tch
bb cc dd ff gg hh kk ll mm
nn pp rr ss tt vv ww zz

Vowel Chunks
aa ae ai ao au aw ay
ea ee ei eo ew ey eau
ia ie ii io iu
oa oe oi oo ou ow oy
ua ue ui uo uy

Wild Tales

Copywork

Copy the story on the lines below. Then mark the same letter patterns that you marked on the printed passage. Look at the previous page if you need help finding the chunks.

Can you guess how howler monkeys got their name? They howl in the morning and in the evening.

Wild Tales **29A**

29B
Vowel, Bossy r, and Consonant Chunks; Endings, Silent Letters

Today's Activities:

☐ Shared reading   ☐ Chunking (**vowel chunks**, **Bossy *r* chunks**, **consonant chunks**, **endings**, **silent letters**)   ☐ Copywork

Can you guess how howler monkeys got their name? They howl in the morning and in the evening. People can hear the howls up to three miles away. Some people think the males are the loudest animals on land.

Endings
-ed -es -ful -ing -ly

Bossy r Chunks
ar er ir or ur

Consonant Chunks
ch	gh	ph	sh	th	wh			
gn	kn	qu	wr	dg	ck	tch		
bb	cc	dd	ff	gg	hh	kk	ll	mm
nn	pp	rr	ss	tt	vv	ww	zz	

Vowel Chunks
aa	ae	ai	ao	au	aw	ay
ea	ee	ei	eo	ew	ey	eau
ia	ie	ii	io	iu		
oa	oe	oi	oo	ou	ow	oy
ua	ue	ui	uo	uy		

126

Wild Tales

Copywork

Copy the story on the lines below. Then mark the same letter patterns that you marked on the printed passage. Look at the previous page if you need help finding the chunks.

People can hear the howls

up to three miles away. Some

people think the males are the

loudest animals on land.

Wild Tales **29B**

29C

Vowel, Bossy *r*, and Consonant Chunks; Endings, Silent Letters

Today's Activities:

☐ Shared reading ☐ Chunking (<u>vowel chunks</u>, <u>Bossy *r* chunks</u>, <u>consonant chunks</u>, <u>endings</u>, <u>silent letters</u>) ☐ Copywork

Can you guess how howler monkeys got their name? They howl in the morning and in the evening. People can hear the howls up to three miles away. Some people think the males are the loudest animals on land.

Endings
-ed -es -ful -ing -ly

Bossy r Chunks
ar er ir or ur

Consonant Chunks
ch gh ph sh th wh
gn kn qu wr dg ck tch
bb cc dd ff gg hh kk ll mm
nn pp rr ss tt vv ww zz

Vowel Chunks
aa ae ai ao au aw ay
ea ee ei eo ew ey eau
ia ie ii io iu
oa oe oi oo ou ow oy
ua ue ui uo uy

● WHERE BLACK HOWLER MONKEYS LIVE

Wild Tales

Copywork

Copy the story on the lines below. Then mark the same letter patterns that you marked on the printed passage. Look at the previous page if you need help finding the chunks.

Can you guess how howler

monkeys got their name?

They howl in the morning and

in the evening.

29D Vowel, Bossy *r*, and Consonant Chunks; Endings, Silent Letters

Today's Activities:

☐ Shared reading ☐ Chunking (**vowel chunks**, **Bossy *r* chunks**, **consonant chunks**, **endings**, **silent letters**) ☐ Dictation

Can you guess how howler monkeys got their name? They howl in the morning and in the evening. People can hear the howls up to three miles away. Some people think the males are the loudest animals on land.

Endings
-ed -es -ful -ing -ly

Bossy r Chunks
ar er ir or ur

Consonant Chunks
ch gh ph sh th wh
gn kn qu wr dg ck tch
bb cc dd ff gg hh kk ll mm
nn pp rr ss tt vv ww zz

Vowel Chunks
aa ae ai ao au aw ay
ea ee ei eo ew ey eau
ia ie ii io iu
oa oe oi oo ou ow oy
ua ue ui uo uy

Wild Tales

No Rule Day

Draw a picture of the story or write your own story. Be creative and have fun.

29E Vowel, Bossy *r*, and Consonant Chunks; Endings, Silent Letters

Today's Activities:

☐ Shared reading   ☐ Chunking (vowel chunks, Bossy *r* chunks, consonant chunks, endings, silent letters)   ☐ Dictation

---

Can you guess how howler monkeys got their name? They howl in the morning and in the evening. People can hear the howls up to three miles away. Some people think the males are the loudest animals on land.

Endings
-ed -es -ful -ing -ly

Bossy r Chunks
ar er ir or ur

Consonant Chunks
ch gh ph sh th wh
gn kn qu wr dg ck tch
bb cc dd ff gg hh kk ll mm
nn pp rr ss tt vv ww zz

Vowel Chunks
aa ae ai ao au aw ay
ea ee ei eo ew ey eau
ia ie ii io iu
oa oe oi oo ou ow oy
ua ue ui uo uy

Wild Tales

Dictation

Turn the page to write this week's story from dictation.

Wild Tales **29E**

Write this week's story from dictation. Take your time and ask for help if you need it.

Can

I spelled _____ words correctly.

30A
Vowel, Bossy *r*, and Consonant Chunks; Silent Letters

See Lesson 30 in the Instructor's Handbook for instructions and tips.

Today's Activities:

☐ Shared reading ☐ Chunking (<u>vowel chunks</u>, <u>Bossy *r* chunks</u>, <u>consonant chunks</u>, <u>silent letters</u>) ☐ Copywork

Squirrels around the world use their tails in many ways. Tails can help them balance in trees. When some squirrels are scared, they fluff and wave their tails to look bigger and stronger. When it is cold, a squirrel can use its tail to keep warm. When it is hot, a squirrel can flip its tail over its back for shade.

Consonant Chunks

ch	gh	ph	sh	th	wh		
gn	kn	qu	wr	dg	ck	tch	
bb	cc	dd	ff	gg	hh	kk	ll	mm
nn	pp	rr	ss	tt	vv	ww	zz

Vowel Chunks

aa	ae	ai	ao	au	aw	ay
ea	ee	ei	eo	ew	ey	eau
ia	ie	ii	io	iu		
oa	oe	oi	oo	ou	ow	oy
ua	ue	ui	uo	uy		

Bossy r Chunks

ar	er	ir	or	ur

Wild Tales

Copywork

Copy the story on the lines below. Then mark the same letter patterns that you marked on the printed passage. Look at the previous page if you need help finding the chunks.

Squirrels use their tails in

S

many ways. Tails help them

m

balance in trees. When some

b

squirrels are scared, they fluff

s

Wild Tales **30A**

30B Vowel, Bossy *r*, and Consonant Chunks; Silent Letters

Today's Activities:

☐ Shared reading ☐ Chunking (**vowel chunks**, **Bossy *r* chunks**, **consonant chunks**, **silent letters**) ☐ Copywork

---

Squirrels around the world use their tails in many ways. Tails can help them balance in trees. When some squirrels are scared, they fluff and wave their tails to look bigger and stronger. When it is cold, a squirrel can use its tail to keep warm. When it is hot, a squirrel can flip its tail over its back for shade.

Consonant Chunks

ch	gh	ph	sh	th	wh	
gn	kn	qu	wr	dg	ck	tch
bb	cc	dd	ff	gg	hh	kk	ll	mm
nn	pp	rr	ss	tt	vv	ww	zz

Vowel Chunks

aa	ae	ai	ao	au	aw	ay
ea	ee	ei	eo	ew	ey	eau
ia	ie	ii	io	iu		
oa	oe	oi	oo	ou	ow	oy
ua	ue	ui	uo	uy		

Bossy r Chunks

ar er ir or ur

Wild Tales

Copywork

Copy the story on the lines below. Then mark the same letter patterns that you marked on the printed passage. Look at the previous page if you need help finding the chunks.

When some squirrels are

scared, they fluff and wave

their tails to look bigger and

stronger. When it is cold,

30C Vowel, Bossy r, and Consonant Chunks; Silent Letters

Today's Activities:

☐ Shared reading ☐ Chunking (**vowel chunks**, **Bossy r chunks**, **consonant chunks**, **silent letters**) ☐ Copywork

Squirrels around the world use their tails in many ways. Tails can help them balance in trees. When some squirrels are scared, they fluff and wave their tails to look bigger and stronger. When it is cold, a squirrel can use its tail to keep warm. When it is hot, a squirrel can flip its tail over its back for shade.

Consonant Chunks

ch	gh	ph	sh	th	wh	
gn	kn	qu	wr	dg	ck	tch
bb	cc	dd	ff	gg	hh	kk	ll	mm
nn	pp	rr	ss	tt	vv	ww	zz

Vowel Chunks

aa	ae	ai	ao	au	aw	ay
ea	ee	ei	eo	ew	ey	eau
ia	ie	ii	io	iu		
oa	oe	oi	oo	ou	ow	oy
ua	ue	ui	uo	uy		

Bossy r Chunks

ar	er	ir	or	ur

140 *Wild Tales*

Copywork

Copy the story on the lines below. Then mark the same letter patterns that you marked on the printed passage. Look at the previous page if you need help finding the chunks.

When it is cold, a squirrel can use its tail to keep warm. When it is hot, a squirrel can flip its tail over its back for shade.

30D
Vowel, Bossy *r*, and Consonant Chunks; Silent Letters

Today's Activities:

☐ Shared reading   ☐ Chunking (**vowel chunks**, **Bossy *r* chunks**, **consonant chunks**, **silent letters**)   ☐ No Rule Day

Squirrels around the world use their tails in many ways. Tails can help them balance in trees. When some squirrels are scared, they fluff and wave their tails to look bigger and stronger. When it is cold, a squirrel can use its tail to keep warm. When it is hot, a squirrel can flip its tail over its back for shade.

Consonant Chunks

ch	gh	ph	sh	th	wh		
gn	kn	qu	wr	dg	ck	tch	
bb	cc	dd	ff	gg	hh	kk	ll	mm
nn	pp	rr	ss	tt	vv	ww	zz

Vowel Chunks

aa	ae	ai	ao	au	aw	ay
ea	ee	ei	eo	ew	ey	eau
ia	ie	ii	io	iu		
oa	oe	oi	oo	ou	ow	oy
ua	ue	ui	uo	uy		

Bossy r Chunks

| ar | er | ir | or | ur |

Wild Tales

No Rule Day

Draw a picture of the story or write your own story. Be creative and have fun.

30E
Vowel, Bossy r, and Consonant Chunks; Silent Letters

Today's Activities:

☐ Shared reading ☐ Chunking (<u>vowel chunks</u>, <u>Bossy r chunks</u>, <u>consonant chunks</u>, <u>silent letters</u>) ☐ Dictation

---

Squirrels around the world use their tails in many ways. Tails can help them balance in trees. When some squirrels are scared, they fluff and wave their tails to look bigger and stronger. When it is cold, a squirrel can use its tail to keep warm. When it is hot, a squirrel can flip its tail over its back for shade.

CALIFORNIA GROUND SQUIRREL

EURASIAN RED SQUIRREL

CAPE GROUND SQUIRREL

EASTERN GRAY SQUIRREL

Consonant Chunks

ch	gh	ph	sh	th	wh		
gn	kn	qu	wr	dg	ck	tch	
bb	cc	dd	ff	gg	hh	kk	ll	mm
nn	pp	rr	ss	tt	vv	ww	zz

Vowel Chunks

aa	ae	ai	ao	au	aw	ay
ea	ee	ei	eo	ew	ey	eau
ia	ie	ii	io	iu		
oa	oe	oi	oo	ou	ow	oy
ua	ue	ui	uo	uy		

Bossy r Chunks

ar	er	ir	or	ur

Wild Tales

Dictation

Turn the page to write this week's story from dictation.

Write this week's story from dictation. Take your time and ask for help if you need it.

Squirrels

31A All Letter Patterns

See Lesson 31 in the Instructor's Handbook for instructions and tips.

Today's Activities:

☐ Shared reading   ☐ Chunking (vowel chunks, Bossy *r* chunks, consonant chunks, Tricky *y* Guy, endings, silent letters)   ☐ Copywork

Did you ever fix dinner while floating on your back? That's what the sea otter does. It gathers clams and puts them into pouches under its front legs. Then it swims to the surface. As it floats, the otter puts a flat rock on its chest. It knocks the clam against the rock to open it. Dinner's ready!

Vowel Chunks

aa	ae	ai	ao	au	aw	ay
ea	ee	ei	eo	ew	ey	eau
ia	ie	ii	io	iu		
oa	oe	oi	oo	ou	ow	oy
ua	ue	ui	uo	uy		

Bossy r Chunks

ar   er   ir   or   ur

Endings

-ed   -es   -ful   -ing   -ly

Consonant Chunks

ch	gh	ph	sh	th	wh	
gn	kn	qu	wr	dg	ck	tch
bb	cc	dd	ff	gg	hh	kk	ll	mm
nn	pp	rr	ss	tt	vv	ww	zz	

148   *Wild Tales*

Copywork

Copy the story on the lines below. Then mark all of the letter patterns you have learned. Look at the previous page if you need help finding the chunks.

Did you ever fix dinner while

floating on your back? That's what

the sea otter does. It gathers

clams and puts them into pouches

Wild Tales **31A**

31B All Letter Patterns

Today's Activities:

☐ Shared reading ☐ Chunking (vowel chunks, Bossy *r* chunks, consonant chunks, Tricky *y* Guy, endings, silent letters) ☐ Copywork

Did you ever fix dinner while floating on your back? That's what the sea otter does. It gathers clams and puts them into pouches under its front legs. Then it swims to the surface. As it floats, the otter puts a flat rock on its chest. It knocks the clam against the rock to open it. Dinner's ready!

Bossy r Chunks
ar   er   ir   or   ur

Endings
-ed   -es   -ful   -ing   -ly

Vowel Chunks
aa	ae	ai	ao	au	aw	ay
ea	ee	ei	eo	ew	ey	eau
ia	ie	ii	io	iu		
oa	oe	oi	oo	ou	ow	oy
ua	ue	ui	uo	uy		

Consonant Chunks
ch	gh	ph	sh	th	wh		
gn	kn	qu	wr	dg	ck	tch	
bb	cc	dd	ff	gg	hh	kk	ll	mm
nn	pp	rr	ss	tt	vv	ww	zz	

Wild Tales

Copywork

Copy the story on the lines below. Then mark all of the letter patterns you have learned. Look at the previous page if you need help finding the chunks.

It gathers clams and puts them into pouches under its front legs. Then it swims to the surface. As it floats,

31C
All Letter Patterns

Today's Activities:

☐ Shared reading ☐ Chunking (**vowel chunks**, **Bossy *r* chunks**, **consonant chunks**, **Tricky *y* Guy**, **endings**, **silent letters**) ☐ Copywork

Did you ever fix dinner while floating on your back? That's what the sea otter does. It gathers clams and puts them into pouches under its front legs. Then it swims to the surface. As it floats, the otter puts a flat rock on its chest. It knocks the clam against the rock to open it. Dinner's ready!

Vowel Chunks

aa	ae	ai	ao	au	aw	ay
ea	ee	ei	eo	ew	ey	eau
ia	ie	ii	io	iu		
oa	oe	oi	oo	ou	ow	oy
ua	ue	ui	uo	uy		

Bossy r Chunks

ar er ir or ur

Endings

-ed -es -ful -ing -ly

Consonant Chunks

ch	gh	ph	sh	th	wh	
gn	kn	qu	wr	dg	ck	tch
bb	cc	dd	ff	gg	hh	kk	ll	mm
nn	pp	rr	ss	tt	vv	ww	zz	

Wild Tales

Copywork

Copy the story on the lines below. Then mark all of the letter patterns you have learned. Look at the previous page if you need help finding the chunks.

As it floats, the otter puts a flat rock on its chest. It knocks the clam against the rock to open it. Dinner's ready!

Wild Tales 31C

31D All Letter Patterns

Today's Activities:

☐ Shared reading ☐ Chunking (<u>vowel chunks</u>, <u>Bossy *r* chunks</u>, <u>consonant chunks</u>, <u>Tricky *y* Guy</u>, <u>endings</u>, <u>silent letters</u>) ☐ No Rule Day

Did you ever fix dinner while floating on your back? That's what the sea otter does. It gathers clams and puts them into pouches under its front legs. Then it swims to the surface. As it floats, the otter puts a flat rock on its chest. It knocks the clam against the rock to open it. Dinner's ready!

Vowel Chunks

aa	ae	ai	ao	au	aw	ay
ea	ee	ei	eo	ew	ey	eau
ia	ie	ii	io	iu		
oa	oe	oi	oo	ou	ow	oy
ua	ue	ui	uo	uy		

Bossy r Chunks

ar er ir or ur

Endings

-ed -es -ful -ing -ly

Consonant Chunks

ch	gh	ph	sh	th	wh	
gn	kn	qu	wr	dg	ck	tch
bb	cc	dd	ff	gg	hh	kk	ll	mm
nn	pp	rr	ss	tt	vv	ww	zz	

Wild Tales

No Rule Day

Draw a picture of the story or write your own story. Be creative and have fun.

31E All Letter Patterns

Today's Activities:

☐ Shared reading   ☐ Chunking (vowel chunks, Bossy *r* chunks, consonant chunks, Tricky *y* Guy, endings, silent letters)   ☐ Dictation

Did you ever fix dinner while floating on your back? That's what the sea otter does. It gathers clams and puts them into pouches under its front legs. Then it swims to the surface. As it floats, the otter puts a flat rock on its chest. It knocks the clam against the rock to open it. Dinner's ready!

Bossy r Chunks

ar er ir or ur

Endings

-ed -es -ful -ing -ly

Vowel Chunks

aa ae ai ao au aw ay

ea ee ei eo ew ey eau

ia ie ii io iu

oa oe oi oo ou ow oy

ua ue ui uo uy

Consonant Chunks

ch gh ph sh th wh

gn kn qu wr dg ck tch

bb cc dd ff gg hh kk ll mm

nn pp rr ss tt vv ww zz

SEA OTTER

CLAM

MICROSCOPIC PLANKTON

A FOOD CHAIN FOR SEA OTTERS

Wild Tales

Dictation

Turn the page to write this week's story from dictation.

Write this week's story from dictation. Take your time and ask for help if you need it.

Did

32A All Letter Patterns

📖 See Lesson 32 in the Instructor's Handbook for instructions and tips.

Today's Activities:

☐ Shared reading   ☐ Chunking (vowel chunks, Bossy r chunks, consonant chunks, Tricky y Guy, endings, silent letters)   ☐ Copywork

A honeybee finds a new patch of flowers. What does it do? The bee flies back to the hive and starts dancing. The way it moves shows where the food is. The number of times the bee shakes its body tells how far away the food is. Soon the other bees are on their way!

Consonant Chunks

ch	gh	ph	sh	th	wh		
gn	kn	qu	wr	dg	ck	tch	
bb	cc	dd	ff	gg	hh	kk	ll	mm
nn	pp	rr	ss	tt	vv	ww	zz

Vowel Chunks

aa	ae	ai	ao	au	aw	ay
ea	ee	ei	eo	ew	ey	eau
ia	ie	ii	io	iu		
oa	oe	oi	oo	ou	ow	oy
ua	ue	ui	uo	uy		

Bossy r Chunks

ar   er   ir   or   ur

Endings

-ed   -es   -ful   -ing   -ly

Wild Tales

Copywork

Copy the story on the lines below. Then mark all of the letter patterns you have learned. Look at the previous page if you need help finding the chunks.

A honeybee finds a new patch of flowers. What does it do? The bee flies back to the hive and starts dancing.

32B All Letter Patterns

Today's Activities:

☐ Shared reading ☐ Chunking (vowel chunks, Bossy *r* chunks, consonant chunks, Tricky *y* Guy, endings, silent letters) ☐ Copywork

A honeybee finds a new patch of flowers. What does it do? The bee flies back to the hive and starts dancing. The way it moves shows where the food is. The number of times the bee shakes its body tells how far away the food is. Soon the other bees are on their way!

Consonant Chunks

ch	gh	ph	sh	th	wh		
gn	kn	qu	wr	dg	ck	tch	
bb	cc	dd	ff	gg	hh	kk	ll	mm
nn	pp	rr	ss	tt	vv	ww	zz

Vowel Chunks

aa	ae	ai	ao	au	aw	ay
ea	ee	ei	eo	ew	ey	eau
ia	ie	ii	io	iu		
oa	oe	oi	oo	ou	ow	oy
ua	ue	ui	uo	uy		

Bossy r Chunks

ar   er   ir   or   ur

Endings

-ed   -es   -ful   -ing   -ly

Wild Tales

Copywork

Copy the story on the lines below. Then mark all of the letter patterns you have learned. Look at the previous page if you need help finding the chunks.

The way it moves shows where

the food is. The number of times

the bee shakes its body tells how

far away the food is.

32C All Letter Patterns

Today's Activities:

☐ Shared reading   ☐ Chunking (**vowel chunks**, **Bossy *r* chunks**, **consonant chunks**, **Tricky *y* Guy**, **endings**, **silent letters**)   ☐ Copywork

A honeybee finds a new patch of flowers. What does it do? The bee flies back to the hive and starts dancing. The way it moves shows where the food is. The number of times the bee shakes its body tells how far away the food is. Soon the other bees are on their way!

Consonant Chunks

ch	gh	ph	sh	th	wh		
gn	kn	qu	wr	dg	ck	tch	
bb	cc	dd	ff	gg	hh	kk	ll	mm
nn	pp	rr	ss	tt	vv	ww	zz

Vowel Chunks

aa	ae	ai	ao	au	aw	ay
ea	ee	ei	eo	ew	ey	eau
ia	ie	ii	io	iu		
oa	oe	oi	oo	ou	ow	oy
ua	ue	ui	uo	uy		

Bossy r Chunks

ar   er   ir   or   ur

Endings

-ed   -es   -ful   -ing   -ly

Wild Tales

Copywork

Copy the story on the lines below. Then mark all of the letter patterns you have learned. Look at the previous page if you need help finding the chunks.

The number of times the bee shakes its body tells how far away the food is. Soon the other bees are on their way!

Wild Tales 32C

32D All Letter Patterns

See Lesson 32 in the Instructor's Handbook for instructions and tips.

Today's Activities:

☐ Shared reading   ☐ Chunking (vowel chunks, Bossy *r* chunks, consonant chunks, Tricky *y* Guy, endings, silent letters)   ☐ No Rule Day

A honeybee finds a new patch of flowers. What does it do? The bee flies back to the hive and starts dancing. The way it moves shows where the food is. The number of times the bee shakes its body tells how far away the food is. Soon the other bees are on their way!

1	2	3	4
MOVE IN A LINE SHAKING BODY	TURN RIGHT AND GO BACK TO START	MOVE IN THE SAME LINE SHAKING BODY	TURN LEFT AND GO BACK TO START

Consonant Chunks

ch	gh	ph	sh	th	wh	
gn	kn	qu	wr	dg	ck	tch
bb	cc	dd	ff	gg	hh	kk	ll	mm
nn	pp	rr	ss	tt	vv	ww	zz

Vowel Chunks

aa	ae	ai	ao	au	aw	ay
ea	ee	ei	eo	ew	ey	eau
ia	ie	ii	io	iu		
oa	oe	oi	oo	ou	ow	oy
ua	ue	ui	uo	uy		

Bossy r Chunks

ar   er   ir   or   ur

Endings

-ed   -es   -ful   -ing   -ly

166   *Wild Tales*

No Rule Day

Draw a picture of the story or write your own story. Be creative and have fun.

32E All Letter Patterns

Today's Activities:

☐ Shared reading ☐ Chunking (vowel chunks, Bossy r chunks, consonant chunks, Tricky y Guy, endings, silent letters) ☐ Dictation

A honeybee finds a new patch of flowers. What does it do? The bee flies back to the hive and starts dancing. The way it moves shows where the food is. The number of times the bee shakes its body tells how far away the food is. Soon the other bees are on their way!

Consonant Chunks

ch	gh	ph	sh	th	wh		
gn	kn	qu	wr	dg	ck	tch	
bb	cc	dd	ff	gg	hh	kk	ll	mm
nn	pp	rr	ss	tt	vv	ww	zz

Vowel Chunks

aa	ae	ai	ao	au	aw	ay
ea	ee	ei	eo	ew	ey	eau
ia	ie	ii	io	iu		
oa	oe	oi	oo	ou	ow	oy
ua	ue	ui	uo	uy		

Bossy r Chunks

ar er ir or ur

Endings

-ed -es -ful -ing -ly

Wild Tales

Dictation

Turn the page to write this week's story from dictation.

Write this week's story from dictation. Take your time and ask for help if you need it.

A

I spelled _____ words correctly.

33A All Letter Patterns

> See Lesson 33 in the Instructor's Handbook for instructions and tips.

Today's Activities:

☐ Shared reading   ☐ Chunking (vowel chunks, Bossy *r* chunks, consonant chunks, Tricky *y* Guy, endings, silent letters)   ☐ Copywork

Many woodpeckers use their beaks for making holes in tree trunks. They look for tunnels made by bugs under the bark. When the woodpecker finds a tunnel, it pecks a small hole. It quickly puts its long tongue inside. The tongue is sticky and has hooks on the end for catching bugs. The bird can also eat bugs that scurry out of the holes.

Vowel Chunks

aa	ae	ai	ao	au	aw	ay
ea	ee	ei	eo	ew	ey	eau
ia	ie	ii	io	iu		
oa	oe	oi	oo	ou	ow	oy
ua	ue	ui	uo	uy		

Endings

-ed   -es   -ful   -ing   -ly

Bossy r Chunks

ar   er   ir   or   ur

Consonant Chunks

ch	gh	ph	sh	th	wh			
gn	kn	qu	wr	dg	ck	tch		
bb	cc	dd	ff	gg	hh	kk	ll	mm
nn	pp	rr	ss	tt	vv	ww	zz	

Wild Tales

Copywork

Copy the story on the lines below. Then mark all of the letter patterns you have learned. Look at the previous page if you need help finding the chunks.

Many woodpeckers use their

M

beaks for making holes in tree

b

trunks. They look for tunnels

t

made by bugs under the bark.

m

Wild Tales **33A**

33B All Letter Patterns

Today's Activities:

☐ Shared reading ☐ Chunking (vowel chunks, Bossy *r* chunks, consonant chunks, Tricky *y* Guy, endings, silent letters) ☐ Copywork

---

Many woodpeckers use their beaks for making holes in tree trunks. They look for tunnels made by bugs under the bark. When the woodpecker finds a tunnel, it pecks a small hole. It quickly puts its long tongue inside. The tongue is sticky and has hooks on the end for catching bugs. The bird can also eat bugs that scurry out of the holes.

Endings
-ed -es -ful -ing -ly

Bossy r Chunks
ar er ir or ur

Vowel Chunks
aa ae ai ao au aw ay
ea ee ei eo ew ey eau
ia ie ii io iu
oa oe oi oo ou ow oy
ua ue ui uo uy

Consonant Chunks
ch gh ph sh th wh
gn kn qu wr dg ck tch
bb cc dd ff gg hh kk ll mm
nn pp rr ss tt vv ww zz

Wild Tales

Copywork

Copy the story on the lines below. Then mark all of the letter patterns you have learned. Look at the previous page if you need help finding the chunks.

When the woodpecker finds a tunnel, it pecks a small hole. It quickly puts its long tongue inside. The tongue is sticky

33C All Letter Patterns

Today's Activities:

☐ Shared reading   ☐ Chunking (**vowel chunks**, **Bossy *r* chunks**, consonant chunks, Tricky *y* Guy, endings, silent letters)   ☐ Copywork

Many woodpeckers use their beaks for making holes in tree trunks. They look for tunnels made by bugs under the bark. When the woodpecker finds a tunnel, it pecks a small hole. It quickly puts its long tongue inside. The tongue is sticky and has hooks on the end for catching bugs. The bird can also eat bugs that scurry out of the holes.

Vowel Chunks

aa	ae	ai	ao	au	aw	ay
ea	ee	ei	eo	ew	ey	eau
ia	ie	ii	io	iu		
oa	oe	oi	oo	ou	ow	oy
ua	ue	ui	uo	uy		

Endings

-ed -es -ful -ing -ly

Bossy r Chunks

ar er ir or ur

Consonant Chunks

ch	gh	ph	sh	th	wh	
gn	kn	qu	wr	dg	ck	tch
bb	cc	dd	ff	gg	hh	kk	ll	mm
nn	pp	rr	ss	tt	vv	ww	zz

Copywork

Copy the story on the lines below. Then mark all of the letter patterns you have learned. Look at the previous page if you need help finding the chunks.

The tongue is sticky and has hooks on the end for catching bugs. The bird can also eat bugs that scurry out of the holes.

33D All Letter Patterns

Today's Activities:

☐ Shared reading ☐ Chunking (vowel chunks, Bossy r chunks, consonant chunks, Tricky y Guy, endings, silent letters) ☐ No Rule Day

Many woodpeckers use their beaks for making holes in tree trunks. They look for tunnels made by bugs under the bark. When the woodpecker finds a tunnel, it pecks a small hole. It quickly puts its long tongue inside. The tongue is sticky and has hooks on the end for catching bugs. The bird can also eat bugs that scurry out of the holes.

Vowel Chunks

aa	ae	ai	ao	au	aw	ay
ea	ee	ei	eo	ew	ey	eau
ia	ie	ii	io	iu		
oa	oe	oi	oo	ou	ow	oy
ua	ue	ui	uo	uy		

Endings

-ed   -es   -ful   -ing   -ly

Bossy r Chunks

ar   er   ir   or   ur

Consonant Chunks

ch	gh	ph	sh	th	wh			
gn	kn	qu	wr	dg	ck	tch		
bb	cc	dd	ff	gg	hh	kk	ll	mm
nn	pp	rr	ss	tt	vv	ww	zz	

Wild Tales

No Rule Day

Draw a picture of the story or write your own story. Be creative and have fun.

33E All Letter Patterns

Today's Activities:

☐ Shared reading   ☐ Chunking (vowel chunks, Bossy *r* chunks, consonant chunks, Tricky *y* Guy, endings, silent letters)   ☐ Dictation

Many woodpeckers use their beaks for making holes in tree trunks. They look for tunnels made by bugs under the bark. When the woodpecker finds a tunnel, it pecks a small hole. It quickly puts its long tongue inside. The tongue is sticky and has hooks on the end for catching bugs. The bird can also eat bugs that scurry out of the holes.

Endings
-ed   -es   -ful   -ing   -ly

Bossy r Chunks
ar   er   ir   or   ur

Vowel Chunks
aa   ae   ai   ao   au   aw   ay
ea   ee   ei   eo   ew   ey   eau
ia   ie   ii   io   iu
oa   oe   oi   oo   ou   ow   oy
ua   ue   ui   uo   uy

Consonant Chunks
ch   gh   ph   sh   th   wh
gn   kn   qu   wr   dg   ck   tch
bb   cc   dd   ff   gg   hh   kk   ll   mm
nn   pp   rr   ss   tt   vv   ww   zz

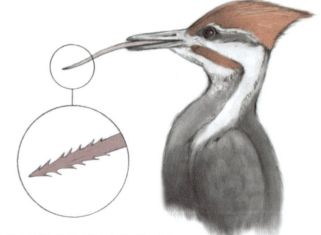

HOOKS ON THE TIP OF A PILEATED WOODPECKER'S TONGUE

Wild Tales

Dictation

Turn the page to write this week's story from dictation.

Write this week's story from dictation. Take your time and ask for help if you need it.

Many

34A All Letter Patterns

See Lesson 34 in the Instructor's Handbook for instructions and tips.

Today's Activities:

☐ Shared reading   ☐ Chunking (vowel chunks, Bossy *r* chunks, consonant chunks, Tricky *y* Guy, endings, silent letters)   ☐ Copywork

Seahorses are fish, but they are not like other fish. Seahorses swim upright. They have a curved neck. They do not have scales. Their fins are very small, so they swim poorly. A seahorse uses its tail to hold onto sea grasses. A group of seahorses is called a herd—just like a herd of horses!

Vowel Chunks

aa	ae	ai	ao	au	aw	ay
ea	ee	ei	eo	ew	ey	eau
ia	ie	ii	io	iu		
oa	oe	oi	oo	ou	ow	oy
ua	ue	ui	uo	uy		

Endings
-ed -es -ful -ing -ly

Bossy r Chunks
ar er ir or ur

Consonant Chunks

ch	gh	ph	sh	th	wh	
gn	kn	qu	wr	dg	ck	tch
bb	cc	dd	ff	gg	hh	kk	ll	mm
nn	pp	rr	ss	tt	vv	ww	zz

Wild Tales

Copywork

Copy the story on the lines below. Then mark all of the letter patterns you have learned. Look at the previous page if you need help finding the chunks.

Seahorses are fish, but they are not like other fish. Seahorses swim upright. They have a curved neck. They do not have scales.

Wild Tales **34A**

34B All Letter Patterns

Today's Activities:

☐ Shared reading   ☐ Chunking (vowel chunks, Bossy *r* chunks, consonant chunks, Tricky *y* Guy, endings, silent letters)   ☐ Copywork

Seahorses are fish, but they are not like other fish. Seahorses swim upright. They have a curved neck. They do not have scales. Their fins are very small, so they swim poorly. A seahorse uses its tail to hold onto sea grasses. A group of seahorses is called a herd—just like a herd of horses!

Vowel Chunks

aa	ae	ai	ao	au	aw	ay
ea	ee	ei	eo	ew	ey	eau
ia	ie	ii	io	iu		
oa	oe	oi	oo	ou	ow	oy
ua	ue	ui	uo	uy		

Endings

-ed -es -ful -ing -ly

Bossy r Chunks

ar er ir or ur

Consonant Chunks

ch	gh	ph	sh	th	wh	
gn	kn	qu	wr	dg	ck	tch
bb	cc	dd	ff	gg	hh	kk	ll	mm
nn	pp	rr	ss	tt	vv	ww	zz	

Wild Tales

Copywork

Copy the story on the lines below. Then mark all of the letter patterns you have learned. Look at the previous page if you need help finding the chunks.

Their fins are very small, so they swim poorly. A seahorse uses its tail to hold onto sea grasses. A group of seahorses is called a herd

34C All Letter Patterns

Today's Activities:

☐ Shared reading   ☐ Chunking (vowel chunks, Bossy *r* chunks, consonant chunks, Tricky *y* Guy, endings, silent letters)   ☐ Copywork

---

Seahorses are fish, but they are not like other fish. Seahorses swim upright. They have a curved neck. They do not have scales. Their fins are very small, so they swim poorly. A seahorse uses its tail to hold onto sea grasses. A group of seahorses is called a herd—just like a herd of horses!

Vowel Chunks

aa	ae	ai	ao	au	aw	ay
ea	ee	ei	eo	ew	ey	eau
ia	ie	ii	io	iu		
oa	oe	oi	oo	ou	ow	oy
ua	ue	ui	uo	uy		

Endings
-ed   -es   -ful   -ing   -ly

Bossy r Chunks
ar   er   ir   or   ur

Consonant Chunks

ch	gh	ph	sh	th	wh	
gn	kn	qu	wr	dg	ck	tch
bb	cc	dd	ff	gg	hh	kk	ll	mm
nn	pp	rr	ss	tt	vv	ww	zz

Wild Tales

Copywork

Copy the story on the lines below. Then mark all of the letter patterns you have learned. Look at the previous page if you need help finding the chunks.

A seahorse uses its tail to hold onto sea grasses. A group of seahorses is called a herd—just like a herd of horses!

34D All Letter Patterns

Today's Activities:

☐ Shared reading ☐ Chunking (vowel chunks, Bossy *r* chunks, consonant chunks, Tricky *y* Guy, endings, silent letters) ☐ No Rule Day

Seahorses are fish, but they are not like other fish. Seahorses swim upright. They have a curved neck. They do not have scales. Their fins are very small, so they swim poorly. A seahorse uses its tail to hold onto sea grasses. A group of seahorses is called a herd—just like a herd of horses!

Vowel Chunks

aa	ae	ai	ao	au	aw	ay
ea	ee	ei	eo	ew	ey	eau
ia	ie	ii	io	iu		
oa	oe	oi	oo	ou	ow	oy
ua	ue	ui	uo	uy		

Endings
-ed   -es   -ful   -ing   -ly

Bossy r Chunks
ar   er   ir   or   ur

Consonant Chunks

ch	gh	ph	sh	th	wh	
gn	kn	qu	wr	dg	ck	tch
bb	cc	dd	ff	gg	hh	kk	ll	mm
nn	pp	rr	ss	tt	vv	ww	zz

Wild Tales

No Rule Day

Draw a picture of the story or write your own story. Be creative and have fun.

34E All Letter Patterns

Today's Activities:

☐ Shared reading ☐ Chunking (vowel chunks, Bossy *r* chunks, consonant chunks, Tricky *y* Guy, endings, silent letters) ☐ Dictation

Seahorses are fish, but they are not like other fish. Seahorses swim upright. They have a curved neck. They do not have scales. Their fins are very small, so they swim poorly. A seahorse uses its tail to hold onto sea grasses. A group of seahorses is called a herd—just like a herd of horses!

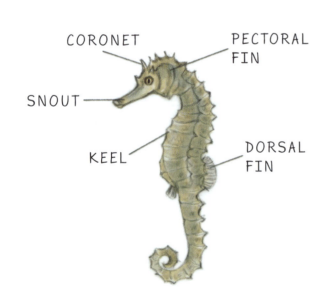

CORONET
PECTORAL FIN
SNOUT
KEEL
DORSAL FIN

Vowel Chunks

aa	ae	ai	ao	au	aw	ay
ea	ee	ei	eo	ew	ey	eau
ia	ie	ii	io	iu
oa	oe	oi	oo	ou	ow	oy
ua	ue	ui	uo	uy

Endings
-ed -es -ful -ing -ly

Bossy r Chunks
ar er ir or ur

Consonant Chunks

ch	gh	ph	sh	th	wh
gn	kn	qu	wr	dg	ck	tch
bb	cc	dd	ff	gg	hh	kk	ll	mm
nn	pp	rr	ss	tt	vv	ww	zz

Wild Tales

Dictation

Turn the page to write this week's story from dictation.

Write this week's story from dictation. Take your time and ask for help if you need it.

Seahorses

I spelled _____ words correctly.

35A All Letter Patterns

See Lesson 35 in the Instructor's Handbook for instructions and tips.

Today's Activities:

☐ Shared reading ☐ Chunking (vowel chunks, Bossy *r* chunks, consonant chunks, Tricky *y* Guy, endings, silent letters) ☐ Copywork

When it is time to lay eggs, a crocodile mother makes a nest. She might dig a hole by a river. When they hatch, the babies call to their mother. They cannot climb out of the hole. The mother picks them up gently in her mouth. Then she carries them to the water.

Consonant Chunks

ch	gh	ph	sh	th	wh	
gn	kn	qu	wr	dg	ck	tch
bb	cc	dd	ff	gg	hh	kk	ll	mm
nn	pp	rr	ss	tt	vv	ww	zz

Vowel Chunks

aa	ae	ai	ao	au	aw	ay
ea	ee	ei	eo	ew	ey	eau
ia	ie	ii	io	iu		
oa	oe	oi	oo	ou	ow	oy
ua	ue	ui	uo	uy		

Endings

-ed -es -ful -ing -ly

Bossy r Chunks

ar er ir or ur

Wild Tales

Copywork

Copy the story on the lines below. Then mark all of the letter patterns you have learned. Look at the previous page if you need help finding the chunks.

When it is time to lay eggs, a crocodile mother makes a nest. She might dig a hole by the river.

35B All Letter Patterns

Today's Activities:

☐ Shared reading   ☐ Chunking (vowel chunks, Bossy *r* chunks, consonant chunks, Tricky *y* Guy, endings, silent letters)   ☐ Copywork

---

When it is time to lay eggs, a crocodile mother makes a nest. She might dig a hole by a river. When they hatch, the babies call to their mother. They cannot climb out of the hole. The mother picks them up gently in her mouth. Then she carries them to the water.

Consonant Chunks

ch	gh	ph	sh	th	wh		
gn	kn	qu	wr	dg	ck	tch	
bb	cc	dd	ff	gg	hh	kk	ll	mm
nn	pp	rr	ss	tt	vv	ww	zz

Vowel Chunks

aa	ae	ai	ao	au	aw	ay
ea	ee	ei	eo	ew	ey	eau
ia	ie	ii	io	iu		
oa	oe	oi	oo	ou	ow	oy
ua	ue	ui	uo	uy		

Endings

-ed   -es   -ful   -ing   -ly

Bossy r Chunks

ar   er   ir   or   ur

Wild Tales

Copywork

Copy the story on the lines below. Then mark all of the letter patterns you have learned. Look at the previous page if you need help finding the chunks.

When they hatch, the babies call to their mother. They cannot climb out of the hole. The mother picks them up gently in her mouth.

35C All Letter Patterns

Today's Activities:

☐ Shared reading   ☐ Chunking (vowel chunks, Bossy *r* chunks, consonant chunks, Tricky *y* Guy, endings, silent letters)   ☐ Copywork

When it is time to lay eggs, a crocodile mother makes a nest. She might dig a hole by a river. When they hatch, the babies call to their mother. They cannot climb out of the hole. The mother picks them up gently in her mouth. Then she carries them to the water.

Consonant Chunks

ch	gh	ph	sh	th	wh			
gn	kn	qu	wr	dg	ck	tch		
bb	cc	dd	ff	gg	hh	kk	ll	mm
nn	pp	rr	ss	tt	vv	ww	zz	

Vowel Chunks

aa	ae	ai	ao	au	aw	ay
ea	ee	ei	eo	ew	ey	eau
ia	ie	ii	io	iu		
oa	oe	oi	oo	ou	ow	oy
ua	ue	ui	uo	uy		

Endings

-ed -es -ful -ing -ly

Bossy r Chunks

ar er ir or ur

Wild Tales

Copywork

Copy the story on the lines below. Then mark all of the letter patterns you have learned. Look at the previous page if you need help finding the chunks.

They cannot climb out of the hole. The mother picks them up gently in her mouth. Then she carries them to the water.

Wild Tales 35C

35D All Letter Patterns

Today's Activities:

☐ Shared reading ☐ Chunking (vowel chunks, Bossy *r* chunks, consonant chunks, Tricky *y* Guy, endings, silent letters) ☐ No Rule Day

---

When it is time to lay eggs, a crocodile mother makes a nest. She might dig a hole by a river. When they hatch, the babies call to their mother. They cannot climb out of the hole. The mother picks them up gently in her mouth. Then she carries them to the water.

Consonant Chunks

ch	gh	ph	sh	th	wh			
gn	kn	qu	wr	dg	ck	tch		
bb	cc	dd	ff	gg	hh	kk	ll	mm
nn	pp	rr	ss	tt	vv	ww	zz	

Vowel Chunks

aa	ae	ai	ao	au	aw	ay
ea	ee	ei	eo	ew	ey	eau
ia	ie	ii	io	iu		
oa	oe	oi	oo	ou	ow	oy
ua	ue	ui	uo	uy		

Endings
-ed -es -ful -ing -ly

Bossy r Chunks
ar er ir or ur

Wild Tales

No Rule Day

Draw a picture of the story or write your own story. Be creative and have fun.

35E All Letter Patterns

Today's Activities:

☐ Shared reading   ☐ Chunking (vowel chunks, Bossy *r* chunks, consonant chunks, Tricky *y* Guy, endings, silent letters)   ☐ Dictation

When it is time to lay eggs, a crocodile mother makes a nest. She might dig a hole by a river. When they hatch, the babies call to their mother. They cannot climb out of the hole. The mother picks them up gently in her mouth. Then she carries them to the water.

Consonant Chunks

ch	gh	ph	sh	th	wh		
gn	kn	qu	wr	dg	ck	tch	
bb	cc	dd	ff	gg	hh	kk	ll	mm
nn	pp	rr	ss	tt	vv	ww	zz

CROCODILE EGG	CHICKEN EGG
SOFT SHELL NEST IS BURIED HEATED BY GROUND CLEAR TURNING WHITE	HARD SHELL NEST ABOVE GROUND HEATED BY HEN VARIOUS COLORS

Vowel Chunks

aa	ae	ai	ao	au	aw	ay
ea	ee	ei	eo	ew	ey	eau
ia	ie	ii	io	iu		
oa	oe	oi	oo	ou	ow	oy
ua	ue	ui	uo	uy		

Endings
-ed   -es   -ful   -ing   -ly

Bossy r Chunks
ar   er   ir   or   ur

Wild Tales

Dictation

Turn the page to write this week's story from dictation.

Write this week's story from dictation. Take your time and ask for help if you need it.

When

36A All Letter Patterns

> See Lesson 36 in the Instructor's Handbook for instructions and tips.

Today's Activities:

☐ Shared reading ☐ Chunking (vowel chunks, Bossy *r* chunks, consonant chunks, Tricky *y* Guy, endings, silent letters) ☐ Copywork

The giant panda is a kind of bear. It lives in the country of China. Tall bamboo plants grow there. This is mostly what the giant panda eats. The panda has to eat a lot of bamboo. Giant pandas spend about half of each day just eating!

■ PLACES WHERE GIANT PANDAS LIVE

Consonant Chunks

ch	gh	ph	sh	th	wh	
gn	kn	qu	wr	dg	ck	tch
bb	cc	dd	ff	gg	hh	kk	ll	mm
nn	pp	rr	ss	tt	vv	ww	zz	

Vowel Chunks

aa	ae	ai	ao	au	aw	ay
ea	ee	ei	eo	ew	ey	eau
ia	ie	ii	io	iu		
oa	oe	oi	oo	ou	ow	oy
ua	ue	ui	uo	uy		

Endings

-ed -es -ful -ing -ly

Bossy r Chunks

ar er ir or ur

Wild Tales

Copywork

Copy the story on the lines below. Then mark all of the letter patterns you have learned. Look at the previous page if you need help finding the chunks.

The giant panda is a kind

of bear. It lives in the

country of China. Tall

bamboo plants grow there.

36B All Letter Patterns

Today's Activities:

☐ Shared reading ☐ Chunking (vowel chunks, Bossy *r* chunks, consonant chunks, Tricky *y* Guy, endings, silent letters) ☐ Copywork

---

The giant panda is a kind of bear. It lives in the country of China. Tall bamboo plants grow there. This is mostly what the giant panda eats. The panda has to eat a lot of bamboo. Giant pandas spend about half of each day just eating!

Consonant Chunks

ch	gh	ph	sh	th	wh		
gn	kn	qu	wr	dg	ck	tch	
bb	cc	dd	ff	gg	hh	kk	ll	mm
nn	pp	rr	ss	tt	vv	ww	zz

Vowel Chunks

aa	ae	ai	ao	au	aw	ay
ea	ee	ei	eo	ew	ey	eau
ia	ie	ii	io	iu		
oa	oe	oi	oo	ou	ow	oy
ua	ue	ui	uo	uy		

Endings
-ed -es -ful -ing -ly

Bossy r Chunks
ar er ir or ur

Wild Tales

Copywork

Copy the story on the lines below. Then mark all of the letter patterns you have learned. Look at the previous page if you need help finding the chunks.

Tall bamboo plants grow there. This is mostly what the giant panda eats. The panda has to eat a lot of bamboo.

Wild Tales 36B

36C All Letter Patterns

Today's Activities:

☐ Shared reading ☐ Chunking (<u>vowel chunks</u>, <u>Bossy r chunks</u>, <u>consonant chunks</u>, <u>Tricky y Guy</u>, <u>endings</u>, <u>silent letters</u>) ☐ Copywork

The giant panda is a kind of bear. It lives in the country of China. Tall bamboo plants grow there. This is mostly what the giant panda eats. The panda has to eat a lot of bamboo. Giant pandas spend about half of each day just eating!

Consonant Chunks

ch	gh	ph	sh	th	wh	
gn	kn	qu	wr	dg	ck	tch
bb	cc	dd	ff	gg	hh	kk	ll	mm
nn	pp	rr	ss	tt	vv	ww	zz

Vowel Chunks

aa	ae	ai	ao	au	aw	ay
ea	ee	ei	eo	ew	ey	eau
ia	ie	ii	io	iu		
oa	oe	oi	oo	ou	ow	oy
ua	ue	ui	uo	uy		

Endings

-ed -es -ful -ing -ly

Bossy r Chunks

ar er ir or ur

Wild Tales

Copywork

Copy the story on the lines below. Then mark all of the letter patterns you have learned. Look at the previous page if you need help finding the chunks.

The panda has to eat a lot of bamboo. Giant pandas spend about half of each day just eating!

Wild Tales **36C**

36D   All Letter Patterns

Today's Activities:

☐ Shared reading   ☐ Chunking (<u>vowel chunks</u>, <u>Bossy *r* chunks</u>, <u>consonant chunks</u>, <u>Tricky *y* Guy</u>, <u>endings</u>, <u>silent letters</u>)   ☐ No Rule Day

The giant panda is a kind of bear. It lives in the country of China. Tall bamboo plants grow there. This is mostly what the giant panda eats. The panda has to eat a lot of bamboo. Giant pandas spend about half of each day just eating!

Consonant Chunks

ch	gh	ph	sh	th	wh		
gn	kn	qu	wr	dg	ck	tch	
bb	cc	dd	ff	gg	hh	kk	ll	mm
nn	pp	rr	ss	tt	vv	ww	zz

Vowel Chunks

aa	ae	ai	ao	au	aw	ay
ea	ee	ei	eo	ew	ey	eau
ia	ie	ii	io	iu		
oa	oe	oi	oo	ou	ow	oy
ua	ue	ui	uo	uy		

Endings
-ed   -es   -ful   -ing   -ly

Bossy r Chunks
ar   er   ir   or   ur

Wild Tales

No Rule Day

Draw a picture of the story or write your own story. Be creative and have fun.

36E All Letter Patterns

Today's Activities:

☐ Shared reading ☐ Chunking (vowel chunks, Bossy *r* chunks, consonant chunks, Tricky *y* Guy, endings, silent letters) ☐ Dictation

The giant panda is a kind of bear. It lives in the country of China. Tall bamboo plants grow there. This is mostly what the giant panda eats. The panda has to eat a lot of bamboo. Giant pandas spend about half of each day just eating!

Consonant Chunks

ch	gh	ph	sh	th	wh		
gn	kn	qu	wr	dg	ck	tch	
bb	cc	dd	ff	gg	hh	kk	mm
nn	pp	rr	ss	tt	vv	ww	zz

Vowel Chunks

aa ae ai ao au aw ay
ea ee ei eo ew ey eau
ia ie ii io iu
oa oe oi oo ou ow oy
ua ue ui uo uy

Endings

-ed -es -ful -ing -ly

Bossy r Chunks

ar er ir or ur

Wild Tales

Dictation

Turn the page to write this week's story from dictation.

Write this week's story from dictation. Take your time and ask for help if you need it.

The